SPELLBOUND

A COMPLETE SPELLING PROGRAMME

BOOK F

FOLENS

Introduction To Teachers and Parents

Spellbound is a Complete Spelling Programme for Primary Schools that supplies children with a variety of word lists.

The lists include: **Phonics** (16 units), Themes (6 units), Commonly Misspelled Words (6 units), **Homophones** (2 units) and **High Frequency Words** (2 units).

It is recommended that children learn 4 spellings from the word list every night.

The *Spellbound* programme adheres to the objectives advocated by the Revised Primary School Curriculum which state that:

In First and Second Class the child is enabled to:
'spell correctly a range of familiar, important and regularly occurring words…'.

In Third and Fourth Class the child is enabled to:
'use a range of aids and strategies [dictionaries, word lists, word searches, spelling checkers, anagrams, regular word patterns]… to improve his/her command of spelling'.

In Fifth and Sixth Class the child is enabled to:
'observe the conventions of grammar, punctuation and spelling in his/her writing'.

The *Spellbound* series of books follows a specific multi-dimensional programme that assists the child in attaining proficiency in spelling.

This is achieved by:

1. Guiding the child in developing their phonological and phonemic awareness in order that they can readily identify sound and letter patterns within words.
2. Using onset and rime strategies to inculcate an awareness of spelling patterns. This is achieved by introducing word families that share the same 'rime', e.g. Page 32, Book F, the family of 'ery' words.
3. Building up a store of High Frequency Words.
4. Highlighting Commonly Misspelled Words and Homophones.
5. Advocating the use of strategies such as: Predict, Look, Say, Cover, Write, Check.
6. Enabling the children to become familiar with common spelling rules, e.g. the fact that the plural of most words is formed by adding 's'.

The *Spellbound* series of books supplies the child with a systematic and consistent experience of spelling and it is this approach which achieves progress and success.

The books are ostensibly aimed at:
Book C: 3rd Class, Book D: 4th Class, Book E: 5th Class and Book F: 6th Class.

Editors:
Deirdre Whelan, Francis Connolly, Donna Garvin
Cover and Book Design:
Philip Ryan
Layout:
Mark McKenna
Illustration:
Tim Hutchinson
Cover Illustration:
Tim Hutchinson & Zara Slattery (G.C.I.)

ISBN 978 1 84131 968 1

© Folens Publishers 2007
Hibernian Industrial Estate,
Greenhills Road, Tallaght, Dublin 24
Produced by Folens Publishers.

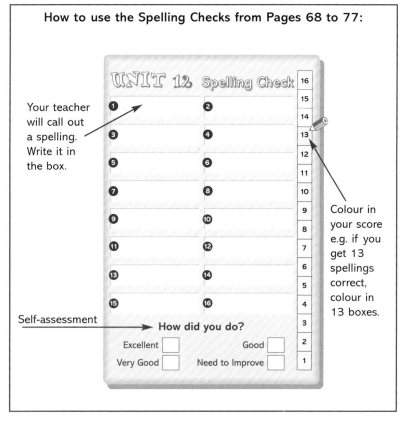

How to use the Spelling Checks from Pages 68 to 77:

UNIT 12 Spelling Check

Your teacher will call out a spelling. Write it in the box.

Colour in your score e.g. if you get 13 spellings correct, colour in 13 boxes.

Self-assessment → How did you do?

Excellent   Good

Very Good   Need to Improve

CONTENTS

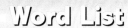

Word List

❶		❷		❸		❹	
there	every	both	goes	these	which	your	some
could	round	does	right	use	write	myself	been

A. Write the missing letters.

1. _th_ ere
2. c _ou_ ld
3. _e_ v _e_ ry
4. r _ou_ nd
5. bo _ot_
6. d _oe_ s
7. _g_ oe _s_
8. ri _ght_
9. _th_ ese
10. u _s_ e
11. whi _c_ h
12. wr _i_ t _e_
13. y _ou_ r
14. my _se_ lf
15. s _o_ m _e_
16. b _ee_ n

B. Unscramble these words. Write them. Find them in the wordsearch.

1. ~~royu~~ _your_
2. ~~emos~~ _some_
3. ~~neeb~~ _been_
4. ~~fyslme~~ _myself_
5. ~~yerev~~ _every_
6. ~~ereth~~ _there_
7. ~~doluc~~ _could_
8. ~~esod~~ _deos_
9. ~~girth~~ _right_
10. ~~thob~~ _both_

```
u e v t z w k h c r w q
w k t q w v h u t c d t
b s d o e s t w h o p p
o o t h e i r w e u p p
w v t v s i b r r l c q
m i v h n a z e e d y j
y v a n x u o k e r o x
s n t c b b r w f n u g
e s o m e e k e v e r y
l j f r j j v p a f i t
f m z v w l t j u h s g
p q b v w a h r i g h t
```

C. Write 10 words from the word list using these letters.
You can use a letter more than once.

v y d m g u n s e t h r e b o

1. _been_
2. _____
3. _____
4. _____
5. _____
6. _____
7. _____
8. _____
9. _____
10. _____

D. Make 3 small words from each word below. You can mix up the letters.

1. your	2. myself	3. round	4. could	5. these
our	_____	_____	_____	_____
_or_	_____	_____	_____	_____
you	_____	_____	_____	_____

E. Crossword. Use the words from the word list.

Across

1. My + self.
3. Communicate on paper.
5. It belongs to you.
7. The two objects.
8. The plural of this.
9. Rhymes with would.

Down

2. All the parts of something.
4. Correct or true.
6. 'Around' minus 'A'.
7. Rhymes with keen.

F. ✗ the 8 incorrect spellings. Write them correctly.

1. yoour ✗
2. some ☐
3. there ☐
4. wich ☐
5. use ☐
6. rownd ☐
7. cuold ☐
8. does ☐
9. bene ☐
10. both ☐
11. these ☐
12. rite ☐
13. every ☐
14. myself ☐
15. gos ☐
16. rihgt ☐

your _____
_____
_____
_____
_____
_____
_____
_____

there
ese

G. Write the missing words. Use the word list.

1. The word _____ rhymes with would.
2. I _____ a letter to my aunt every month.
3. I have _____ ill for the past few days.
4. _____ cloud has a silver lining.
5. I hope I got all the sums _____.
6. My parents are _____ Spanish.
7. I will give you back _____ pen.
8. There is _____ cake left over.
9. Tom found the dog over _____ beside the pond.
10. I couldn't decide _____ kitten to take.

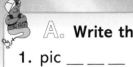

Word List

❶		❷		❸		❹	
picnic	comic	attic	public	traffic	frantic	magnetic	athletic
magic	music	panic	Arctic	elastic	terrific	clinic	fantastic

A. Write the missing letters.

1. pic __ __ __
2. __ __ gic
3. __ __ mic
4. mu __ __ __

5. a __ __ ic
6. __ an __ __
7. pub __ __ __
8. __ __ ct __ __

9. tra __ __ ic
10. el __ __ tic
11. __ __ ant __ __
12. ter __ if __ __ __

13. mag __ __ __ ic
14. __ __ in __ __ __
15. ath __ __ __ __ ic
16. __ __ __ __ __ astic

B. Make 3 small words from each word below. You can mix up the letters.

1. traffic   2. elastic   3. arctic   4. frantic   5. public

cart _____   _____   _____   _____   _____

_____   _____   _____   _____   _____

_____   _____   _____   _____   _____

C. Crossword.

Across

1. Panic stricken.
3. Material that stretches but returns to its original shape.
6. Humorous.
8. Mysterious powers.
9. The production of pleasant sounds.
10. Place where medical treatment is given.

Down

2. A room at the top of a house.
4. Area around the North Pole.
5. A portable meal eaten outdoors.
7. Sudden anxiety.

North Pole

D. Remove a letter (or letters) to make a new word.

1. magnetic = _mane_
2. arctic = _____
3. picnic = _____
4. elastic = _____
5. frantic = _____
6. athletic = _____
7. panic = _____
8. fantastic = _____
9. clinic = _____

E. Write the missing words. Use the word list.

1. We are going to convert our _____ into a bedroom.
2. Only a few people in our class like country _____.
3. I'm going to borrow a book from the _____ library.
4. My canary flew off and I was _____ to find him.
5. I'm going to learn how to do _____ tricks.
6. The fur of the _____ fox turns white in winter.
7. We brought our dog to the veterinary _____.
8. We had a _____ time on holidays this year.
9. Yesterday was a sunny day so we had a _____ in the park.
10. We were late getting home because of the _____ on the motorway.

F. Unscramble these words. Write them. Find them in the wordsearch.

1. cfiraft   _____
2. scatafnti   _____
3. cliicn   _____
4. iefrtirc   _____
5. cgnaemti   _____
6. cicpin   _____
7. titleahc   _____
8. craifnt   _____
9. clatesi   _____
10. ctairc   _____

n	j	u	r	y	y	y	b	e	p	u	f
b	p	i	c	n	i	c	n	l	x	z	i
j	h	t	g	f	i	w	e	a	n	f	h
c	y	b	e	y	d	o	l	s	w	a	A
q	z	b	d	s	a	s	u	t	t	n	r
m	a	g	n	e	t	i	c	i	e	t	c
t	d	b	z	j	h	z	b	c	r	a	t
g	n	i	y	m	l	j	p	c	r	s	i
o	j	j	u	i	e	u	h	d	i	t	c
h	j	d	h	c	t	r	a	f	f	i	c
f	r	a	n	t	i	c	o	e	i	c	o
c	l	i	n	i	c	e	s	r	c	k	m

G. Write the word list in alphabetical order.

1. Arctic   5. _____   9. _____   13. _____
2. _____ 6. _____   10. _____   14. _____
3. _____ 7. _____   11. _____   15. _____
4. _____ 8. _____   12. _____   16. traffic

H. Match the letters. Write the words.

Arc   lic   1. Arctic   ath   tic   7. _____
traf   ic   2. _____   fra   ific   8. _____
clin   stic   3. _____   fantas nic   9. _____
ela   netic   4. _____   pic   letic   10. _____
mag   fic   5. _____   terr   ic   11. _____
pub   tic   6. _____   mag   ntic   12. _____

Word List

❶		❷		❸		❹	
know	laugh	would	their	before	around	once	please
together	eight	those	don't	because	always	again	where

A. Write the missing letters.

1. kn __ __
2. to __ __ __ her
3. la __ __ __
4. __ __ __ ht

5. __ __ uld
6. th __ __ __
7. th __ __ __
8. __ __ n't

9. be __ __ __ e
10. bec __ __ __ __
11. aro __ __ __
12. alw __ __ __

13. o __ __ e
14. a __ __ __ n
15. ple __ __ __
16. wh __ __ __

B. Unscramble these words. Write them. Find them in the wordsearch.

1. hweer   _____
2. inaga   _____
3. slaway   _____
4. refeob   _____
5. dulow   _____
6. ueasebc   _____
7. elepas   _____
8. daronu   _____
9. hagul   _____
10. erith   _____

a	r	o	u	n	d	v	r	j	z	b	a
i	o	g	d	o	j	s	v	p	a	e	z
x	t	r	k	m	x	p	u	w	z	f	w
t	h	e	i	r	i	h	z	d	f	o	k
w	h	e	r	e	r	q	p	d	y	r	o
b	v	i	f	a	g	a	i	n	l	e	h
w	o	u	l	d	x	h	k	i	a	y	p
z	q	f	i	u	j	a	v	a	u	e	l
q	s	w	i	s	w	e	x	t	g	v	e
p	d	f	w	z	h	a	z	p	h	k	a
j	k	s	x	b	e	c	a	u	s	e	s
d	o	l	i	a	l	w	a	y	s	w	e

C. Write 10 words from the word list using these letters. You can use a letter more than once.

p g k n w r i s t h e c n o a r u d e l

1. _____
2. _____
3. _____
4. _____
5. _____
6. _____
7. _____
8. _____
9. _____
10. _____

D. Make 3 small words from each word below. You can mix up the letters.

1. always   2. please   3. around   4. would   5. those

   saw _____   _____   _____   _____   _____

   _____   _____   _____   _____   _____

   _____   _____   _____   _____   _____

Across

2. With another or others.

5. To make happy sounds.

7. Rhymes with there.

9. As a result of.

10. Only one time.

Down

1. To have learned something.

3. A number.

4. At an earlier time.

6. At all times.

8. Once more.

F. ✗ the 8 **incorrect** spellings. Write them correctly.

1. wheyr	✗	9. befour	☐	_____
2. know	☐	10. don't	☐	_____
3. agen	☐	11. luagh	☐	_____
4. together	☐	12. around	☐	_____
5. eight	☐	13. theyre	☐	_____
6. allways	☐	14. once	☐	_____
7. those	☐	15. please	☐	_____
8. beecause	☐	16. wuld	☐	_____

G. **Write the missing words. Use the word list.**

1. I'd like to go _____ the world in eighty days.

2. Just for _____ I'd like to win the lottery!

3. My friend _____ wins the egg and spoon race.

4. I'd love to go ice-skating _____.

5. I need a new coat _____ my old one is too small.

6. Our cat and dog do not get on very well _____.

7. Ben found my pencil so I _____ need to get a new one.

8. My cousins brought _____ dog with them on holidays.

9. I read the second book in the trilogy _____ I read the first.

10. I was in Disneyland last year but I _____ love to go again.

UNIT 4

Word List

❶		❷		❸		❹	
pier	priest	fierce	field	grief	chief	shriek	siege
piece	niece	shield	yield	thief	relief	believe	achieve

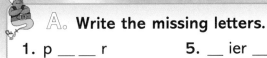

A. Write the missing letters.

1. p __ __ r
2. __ ie __ __
3. pr __ __ st
4. n __ __ ce

5. __ ier __ __
6. sh __ __ ld
7. __ ie __ __
8. y __ __ ld

9. gr __ __ f
10. __ __ ie __
11. ch __ __ f
12. r __ __ ie __

13. shr __ __ k
14. b __ __ ie __ __
15. s __ __ ge
16. a __ __ ie __ __

B. Make 3 small words from each word below. You can mix up the letters.

1. priest   2. fierce   3. believe   4. achieve   5. shield

step ____   _____   _____   _____   _____

_____   _____   _____   _____   _____

_____   _____   _____   _____   _____

C. Crossword.

Across

3. Opposite to nephew.
4. Military operation.
6. Large area of land.
7. Section of.
8. A ruler or leader.

Down

1. Give way.
2. Feel certain of.
4. Yell.
5. Sorrow.
7. A structure extending from the shore to the water.

D. Remove a letter (or letters) to make a new word.

1. priest = rest
2. shield = _____
3. believe = _____

4. siege = _____
5. achieve = _____
6. niece = _____

7. relief = _____
8. thief = _____
9. fierce = _____

Write the missing words. Use the word list.

1. There was a huge bull snorting at the end of the _____.
2. I tried to _____ my little brother from the driving rain.
3. The boat was moored at the end of the _____.
4. I'd like to _____ the best result I can in the test.
5. The lion bared his teeth and looked very _____.
6. I find it hard to _____ I lost my pocket money.
7. The _____ of police took charge of the investigation.
8. The _____ tripped over the cat and set off the alarm.
9. The _____ was over and the hostages were released.
10. I felt great _____ when I saw the ambulance coming.

F. **Unscramble these words. Write them. Find them in the wordsearch.**

1. eigse   _____
2. hecfi   _____
3. vlebeie   _____
4. cirefe   _____
5. khesir   _____
6. ceaeivh   _____
7. trepsi   _____
8. dhesli   _____
9. eicne   _____
10. flerie   _____

g	h	p	d	v	o	t	e	h	p	q	t
t	w	a	q	c	h	i	e	f	r	f	h
r	r	e	l	i	e	f	s	r	i	j	r
l	k	k	t	z	q	o	u	u	e	f	j
x	b	e	l	i	e	v	e	f	s	u	x
z	i	s	h	i	e	l	d	i	t	m	m
o	e	k	c	y	i	f	i	e	x	k	s
n	i	e	c	e	p	t	a	r	e	t	h
y	v	s	i	e	g	e	k	c	w	v	r
a	c	h	i	e	v	e	d	e	a	p	i
x	u	i	a	y	h	c	q	y	i	i	e
u	b	d	e	b	a	n	m	z	t	l	k

G. **Write the word list in alphabetical order.**

1. <u>achieve</u>   5. _____   9. _____   13. _____
2. _____   6. _____   10. _____   14. _____
3. _____   7. _____   11. _____   15. _____
4. _____   8. _____   12. _____   16. <u>yield</u>

H. **Match the letters. Write the words.**

p	iest	1. _____		ach	lieve	7. _____
rel	ge	2. _____		ch	ield	8. _____
pr	ief	3. _____		p	ieve	9. _____
fie	ier	4. _____		be	iece	10. _____
sie	ef	5. _____		shr	ief	11. _____
gri	ld	6. _____		sh	iek	12. _____

Word List

crocus	❶ carnation	geranium	❷ poppy	chestnut	❸ maple	palm	❹ poplar
daffodil	tulip	orchid	dahlia	birch	cedar	yew	sycamore

A. Write the missing letters.

1. cr __ __ us
2. da __ __ __ dil
3. car __ __ __ ion
4. t __ __ ip
5. ger __ __ __ um
6. or __ __ id
7. po __ __ y
8. da __ __ ia
9. ch __ __ __ nut
10. b __ __ ch
11. map __ __
12. ced __ __
13. pa __ m
14. y __ __
15. pop __ __ __
16. s __ __ __ more

B. Crossword.

Across

1. Automobile + country.
2. This flower is usually red.
5. It has two lips!
7. A flower that sounds like a place for growing apples.
8. The seeds of this tree have wings.

Down

1. This tree produces a hard brown nut.
2. A tree and part of your hand.
3. Sounds like a popular tree.
4. Not 'you'! It's the tree!
6. An evergreen tree with sweet-smelling wood.

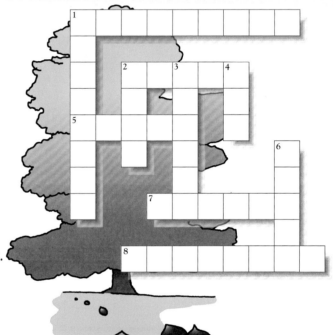

C. Write the word list in alphabetical order.

1. birch
2. _____
3. _____
4. _____
5. _____
6. _____
7. _____
8. _____
9. _____
10. _____
11. _____
12. _____
13. _____
14. _____
15. _____
16. yew

D. Write a word from the word list that contains these letters.

1. ar   poplar
2. or   _____
3. ah   _____
4. es   _____
5. ir   _____
6. an   _____
7. at   _____
8. oc   _____
9. am   _____

E. **Unscramble these words. Write them. Find them in the wordsearch.**

1. lpma _____
2. redca _____
3. anermuig _____
4. macreoys _____
5. yoppp _____
6. cihdro _____
7. cbrhi _____
8. cscuor _____
9. dolifadf _____
10. loprap _____

i	d	a	f	f	o	d	i	l	m	d	o
i	s	d	o	j	j	b	p	o	p	p	y
c	i	w	f	u	k	i	m	h	m	p	w
x	j	c	q	u	j	r	z	p	a	l	m
u	s	v	t	k	g	c	m	t	n	p	f
n	t	s	q	r	e	h	k	i	j	o	i
c	e	d	a	r	r	k	o	t	i	p	f
d	r	s	y	c	a	m	o	r	e	l	u
m	n	w	u	d	n	q	n	v	u	a	z
g	f	c	w	d	i	f	p	r	n	r	t
h	o	p	j	n	u	o	r	c	h	i	d
z	m	f	j	y	m	c	r	o	c	u	s

F. **Remove a letter (or letters) to make a new word.**

1. daffodil = _foil_
2. maple = _____
3. orchid = _____
4. geranium = _____
5. tulip = _____
6. chestnut = _____
7. ccdar = _____
8. carnation = _____
9. sycamore = _____

G. **Find 10 words from the word list on the kite. Write them.**

1. _tulip_
2. _____
3. _____
4. _____
5. _____
6. _____
7. _____
8. _____
9. _____
10. _____

H. **Match the letters. Write the words.**

croc	lia	1. _____	geran	py	7. _____
orch	m	2. _____	ced	w	8. _____
pal	ip	3. _____	bir	lar	9. _____
dah	le	4. _____	pop	ar	10. _____
tul	us	5. _____	ye	ium	11. _____
map	id	6. _____	pop	ch	12. _____

13

Word List

❶		❷		❸		❹	
bored	grate	steal	allowed	sweet	medal	beach	course
board	great	steel	aloud	suite	meddle	beech	coarse

A. Write the missing letters.

1. bo __ __ __
2. __ __ ard
3. gr __ __ __
4. __ __ ea __

5. st __ __ l
6. __ __ ee __
7. a __ __ ow __ __
8. __ l __ __ d

9. sw __ __ t
10. s __ __ t __
11. med __ __
12. __ __ dd __ __

13. b __ __ ch
14. __ ee __ __
15. c __ __ r __ e
16. __ oa __ se

B. Crossword.

Across

1. Rob.
4. Direction or route.
6. Strand.
8. Very good.
9. Interfere.

Down

1. A type of metal.
2. Audibly, not silently.
3. A deciduous tree.
5. Opposite to bitter.
7. Rough.

C. Write a sentence for each word.

1. board _____
2. great _____
3. steal _____
4. aloud _____
5. suite _____
6. meddle _____
7. beech _____
8. course _____

D. Write the word list in alphabetical order.

1. <u>allowed</u>
2. _____
3. _____
4. _____
5. _____
6. _____
7. _____
8. _____
9. _____
10. _____
11. _____
12. _____
13. _____
14. _____
15. _____
16. <u>sweet</u>

E. Read the clues. Write the word. Find it in the wordsearch.

1. Play chess on one.   <u>board</u>
2. A large tree.   _____
3. Given as an award.   _____
4. Noisily.   _____
5. Part of a fireplace.   _____
6. Play golf on one.   _____
7. It is hard and grey.   _____
8. Set of furniture.   _____

e	k	v	t	f	s	t	l	i	m	k	y
m	r	n	l	y	u	s	t	e	c	l	m
k	o	w	m	c	o	u	r	s	e	d	b
k	t	s	d	k	n	e	q	k	p	o	e
q	g	y	s	u	i	t	e	z	v	y	e
w	k	w	l	w	k	r	f	g	i	b	c
a	l	o	u	d	b	e	f	o	g	d	h
b	o	a	r	d	t	t	s	c	w	j	x
m	e	d	a	l	r	a	q	c	a	h	v
s	f	m	g	r	g	r	a	t	e	s	k

F. Remove a letter (or letters) to make a new word.

1. ~~c~~oarse = <u>case</u>
2. suite = _____
3. allowed = _____
4. board = _____
5. bored = _____
6. great = _____
7. course = _____
8. meddle = _____
9. medal = _____

G. Write the missing words. Use the word list.

1. I wanted to play scrabble but the _____ was missing.
2. My baby brother is always trying to _____ with the computer.
3. The chef began to _____ some cheese over the pizza.
4. My dad is doing a painting _____.
5. We're getting a new _____ of furniture today.
6. The _____ tree loses its leaves in autumn.
7. The trapeze artiste had nerves of _____.
8. My mum sings _____ when she's in the shower.

H. Make 2 small words from each word below. You can mix up the letters.

1. steal   2. medal   3. beach   4. course   5. suite

<u>last</u>   _____   _____   _____   _____

_____   _____   _____   _____   _____

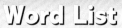

Word List

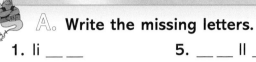

❶		❷		❸		❹	
liar	altar	collar	beggar	grammar	popular	singular	regular
pillar	dollar	cellar	burglar	sugar	vinegar	muscular	particular

A. Write the missing letters.

1. li __ __
2. __ __ ll __ __
3. alt __ __
4. do __ __ ar

5. __ __ ll __ __
6. ce __ __ ar
7. __ __ gg __ __
8. bur __ __ ar

9. gra __ __ ar
10. su __ __ __
11. __ __ __ ul __ __
12. vin __ __ ar

13. sing __ __ ar
14. __ __ scul __ __
15. reg __ __ ar
16. __ __ rtic __ lar

B. Make 3 small words from each word below. You can mix up the letters.

1. pillar   2. dollar   3. beggar   4. regular   5. particular

rail _____   _____   _____   _____   _____

_____   _____   _____   _____   _____

_____   _____   _____   _____   _____

C. Crossword.

Across

5. Someone who doesn't tell the truth.
6. A sweet substance.
8. A band of material for around the neck.
9. A storage room under a house.
10. The structure of a language.

Down

1. Part of a church.
2. Specific.
3. Having well-developed muscles.
4. A poor person who lives by asking for food or money.
7. Ordinary.

D. Remove a letter (or letters) to make a new word.

1.   v̶inegar = _near_   3.   beggar = _____   5.   muscular = _____
2.   collar = _____   4.   burglar = _____   6.   particular = _____

E. Write the missing words. Use the word list.

1. The _____ form of the word 'sheep' is 'sheep'.
2. Our cat has a _____ with a bell on it.
3. My sister puts two spoonfuls of _____ in her tea.
4. Our cousins in France have a wine _____.
5. I'm very _____ about the programmes I watch.
6. The American currency is the _____.
7. The actor who plays Tarzan is very _____.
8. The _____ set off the alarm as she tried to enter the house.
9. I used to find English _____ quite difficult but now I think it's easy.
10. The song that was the most _____ last summer is now the most unpopular!

F. Unscramble these words. Write them. Find them in the wordsearch.

1. regabg _____
2. relarug _____
3. rlpirtuaca _____
4. ligusanr _____
5. mraagmr _____
6. aolrpup _____
7. rcausuml _____
8. rurlbag _____
9. aoldlr _____
10. anervgi _____

g	r	a	m	m	a	r	f	c	o	y	v
y	t	d	i	q	l	z	t	i	w	r	c
s	e	q	g	b	u	r	g	l	a	r	e
s	b	p	a	r	t	i	c	u	l	a	r
l	r	e	p	o	p	u	l	a	r	o	d
s	i	n	g	u	l	a	r	z	w	i	o
n	c	u	i	g	l	w	w	s	u	k	l
c	k	v	p	y	a	o	o	k	f	l	l
d	j	z	n	y	l	r	m	c	u	k	a
x	y	y	n	w	v	i	n	e	g	a	r
t	t	j	v	m	u	s	c	u	l	a	r
h	t	r	e	g	u	l	a	r	v	d	n

G. Write the word list in alphabetical order.

1. altar
2. _____
3. _____
4. _____
5. _____
6. _____
7. _____
8. _____
9. _____
10. _____
11. _____
12. _____
13. _____
14. _____
15. _____
16. vinegar

H. Match the letters. Write the words.

coll	gar	1. _____
pop	mar	2. _____
gram	gular	3. _____
beg	ar	4. _____
sin	lar	5. _____
cel	ular	6. _____

part	ular	7. _____
l	cular	8. _____
reg	lar	9. _____
burg	icular	10. _____
mus	gar	11. _____
su	iar	12. _____

Wordlist

yield	❶	condemn	❷ visible	harass	❸ worthwhile	exceed	❹ embarrass
jealous	argument	simply	cemetery	fulfil	desperate	subtle	thorough

A. Write the missing letters.

1. y __ __ ld
2. j __ __ lous
3. v __ __ l __ nce
4. arg __ __ ent

5. cond __ __ n
6. sim __ __ __
7. v __ s __ ble
8. c __ __ et __ ry

9. har __ __ __
10. f __ __ fi __
11. worthw __ __ le
12. desp __ __ __ te

13. ex __ __ __ d
14. su __ tle
15. emb __ __ rass
16. th __ __ oug __

B. Unscramble these words. Write them. Find them in the wordsearch.

1. uenmtgar _____
2. mlpyis _____
3. enmndco _____
4. llffui _____
5. eidly _____
6. tedseprae _____
7. alejsou _____
8. metryeec _____
9. nceeiolv _____
10. sbiievl _____

k	h	r	c	p	c	p	z	d	w	k	a
y	i	e	l	d	s	w	v	e	x	d	e
o	a	v	j	x	s	k	i	s	q	c	t
r	c	u	h	j	j	e	s	p	n	o	p
a	a	w	o	r	u	t	i	e	f	n	s
e	h	r	m	h	a	k	b	r	u	d	i
r	a	e	g	l	z	c	l	a	l	e	m
z	d	s	l	u	h	m	e	t	f	m	p
y	l	h	r	k	m	b	o	e	i	n	l
r	c	e	m	e	t	e	r	y	l	o	y
b	e	v	i	o	l	e	n	c	e	e	v
j	e	a	l	o	u	s	t	t	y	z	d

C. Write 10 words from the word list using these letters. You can use a letter more than once.

e x b i v y r c d t e n u g s u l m b j h p y o a i e

1. _____
2. _____
3. _____
4. _____
5. _____
6. _____
7. _____
8. _____
9. _____
10. _____

D. Make 3 small words from each word below. You can mix up the letters.

1. desperate
2. thorough
3. worthwhile
4. argument
5. cemetery

speed _____

_____

_____

E. Crossword.

Across

1. In a straightforward way.
4. Destructive behaviour.
6. To make someone feel ashamed.
7. Not easy to notice immediately.

Down

2. _ _ _ _ _ _. Right of way!
3. Go beyond the limit.
4. Not invisible!
5. Pester.

F. ✗ the 8 incorrect spellings. Write them correctly.

1. fulfill	☐	9. condemn	☐	______________
2. violance	☐	10. desparate	☐	______________
3. cemetary	☐	11. worthwhile	☐	______________
4. yeild	☐	12. embarass	☐	______________
5. exseed	☐	13. simply	☐	______________
6. jealous	☐	14. thorough	☐	______________
7. subtle	☐	15. harrass	☐	______________
8. argument	☐	16. visible	☐	______________

G. Write the missing words. Use the word list.

1. 'Don't ____________ me,' said the frazzled parent to the child.
2. Drivers are not allowed to ____________ 120 km/h on the motorway.
3. ____________ solves nothing.
4. He gave his apartment a ____________ spring clean.
5. The sign said ' ____________. Right of way'.
6. The beach wasn't ____________ through the mist.
7. The poem contained a very ____________ message.
8. Do not ____________ and you will not be condemned.
9. He was terrified walking past the ____________ so late at night.
10. The children got into an ____________ about who should go first.

uNIT 9

Word List

❶	❷	❸	❹
edge ledge	judge budge	trudge bridge	pledge lodger
hedge wedge	nudge badger	grudge fridge	smudge dredge

A. Write the missing letters.

1. e __ __ __ __
2. __ __ dge
3. le __ __ __ __
4. we __ __ __

5. ju __ __ __ __
6. __ __ __ ge
7. b __ __ ge
8. __ adg __ __

9. tr __ __ ge
10. __ __ ud __ __
11. br __ __ ge
12. __ __ id __ __

13. pl __ __ ge
14. __ __ u __ __ __ __
15. lo __ __ er
16. dr __ __ ge

B. Make 3 small words from each word below. You can mix up the letters.

1. badger   2. trudge   3. pledge   4. fridge   5. smudge

   rage _____   _____   _____   _____   _____

   _____   _____   _____   _____   _____

   _____   _____   _____   _____   _____

C. Crossword.

Across

3. Move slightly.
4. A paying guest.
6. Shortened version of refrigerator.
7. A promise.

Down

1. A nocturnal animal.
2. It has one thick and one thin end.
3. It connects two locations.
4. Narrow surface projecting outwards.
5. A line of shrubs and trees.

D. Remove a letter (or letters) to make a new word.

1. ~~badger~~ = _bag_
2. smudge = _____
3. grudge = _____

4. lodger = _____
5. fridge = _____
6. pledge = _____

7. wedge = _____
8. judge = _____
9. budge = _____

E. Write the missing words. Use the word list.

1. My sister can hold a _____ against me for days on end.

2. My uncle had a _____ in his house for six months.

3. I gave my solemn _____ to uphold the rules of the game.

4. I placed a wooden _____ under the door to keep it open.

5. The _____ gave the prisoner a sentence of four years.

6. Our little kitten has a _____ of black on his head.

7. I decided to _____ my way home through the snow.

8. We need to _____ the canal as it is clogged with weeds and mud.

9. The young seagull stood on the _____ of the cliff and then flew off.

10. My friend fell asleep during the play so I gave her a _____.

F. Unscramble these words. Write them. Find them in the wordsearch.

1. rogled   _____

2. reagbd   _____

3. gerdde   _____

4. grdteu   _____

5. eugsdm   _____

6. erigbd   _____

7. eudggr   _____

8. udgne   _____

9. eigfdr   _____

10. deeg   _____

u	z	f	r	c	v	m	x	i	y	v	l
d	y	t	p	a	g	r	u	d	g	e	q
g	d	r	e	d	g	e	d	m	o	f	m
t	l	t	m	j	n	z	w	o	s	r	e
n	n	a	o	l	b	j	q	l	m	i	d
t	i	m	b	r	i	d	g	e	u	d	g
j	k	h	j	i	c	t	s	x	d	g	e
l	t	b	j	a	y	v	f	h	g	e	t
c	b	a	d	g	e	r	x	i	e	y	g
l	o	d	g	e	r	t	r	u	d	g	e
n	u	d	g	e	o	r	u	t	h	p	l
v	d	r	n	m	u	p	b	v	w	f	j

G. Write the word list in alphabetical order.

1. <u>badger</u>

2. _____

3. _____

4. _____

5. _____

6. _____

7. _____

8. _____

9. _____

10. _____

11. _____

12. _____

13. _____

14. _____

15. _____

16. <u>wedge</u>

H. Match the letters. Write the words.

e	edge	1. _____	sm	edge	7. _____
p	idge	2. _____	d	idge	8. _____
lo	dge	3. _____	b	udge	9. _____
h	ledge	4. _____	w	adger	10. _____
br	ge	5. _____	fr	dge	11. _____
led	dger	6. _____	ju	redge	12. _____

UNIT 10

Word List

pollution ❶ preserve	reuse ❷ habitat	global ❸ endangered	desert ❹ landscape
recycle reduce	natural ozone	plentiful rainforest	scarce environment

A. Write the missing letters.

1. pollut __ __ __
2. re __ __ __ le
3. pre __ __ __ ve
4. red __ __ e
5. r __ __ se
6. nat __ __ al
7. hab __ __ __ __
8. o __ __ __ e
9. gl __ __ al
10. pl __ __ tif __ l
11. __ __ dangered
12. rainf __ __ est
13. d __ __ ert
14. sc __ __ ce
15. land __ __ __ pe
16. __ __ __ ironment

B. Crossword.

Across

1. Wooded area in a tropical climate.
5. The Sahara is an example.
6. The opposite of plentiful.
8. It destroys our environment.
9. To keep something safe or in good condition.

Down

2. Reduce, Reuse, __ __ __ __ __ __ __ __.
3. To lessen or make smaller.
4. Not made by people or machines.
7. A layer of colourless gas that protects us from the sun.

C. Write the word list in alphabetical order.

1. <u>desert</u>
2. _____
3. _____
4. _____
5. _____
6. _____
7. _____
8. _____
9. _____
10. _____
11. _____
12. _____
13. _____
14. _____
15. _____
16. <u>scarce</u>

D. Write a word from the word list that contains these letters.

1. er _____
2. en _____
3. an _____
4. al _____
5. it _____
6. ar _____
7. ai _____
8. ur _____
9. ll _____

E. Unscramble these words. Write them. Find them in the wordsearch.

1. casrec _____
2. cyerlce _____
3. nzeoo _____
4. represev _____
5. tanrula _____
6. nutoilopl _____
7. retsed _____
8. deucer _____
9. loblag _____
10. agndnereed _____

| n a t u r a l o l p o r |
| s c a r c e i z z j s e |
| u i x m r p m o c i t c |
| h o i s a o c n t e p y |
| u y o j v j g e e g r c |
| g l o b a l h l p z e l |
| e n d a n g e r e d s e |
| r e d u c e k h o l e t |
| o z o g k m d e s e r t |
| p v v x l v c v l g v w |
| y s v p w g i b u e e f |
| p o l l u t i o n m t i |

F. Remove a letter (or letters) to make a new word.

1. ~~re~~cycle = cycle
2. habitat = _____
3. desert = _____
4. ozone = _____
5. reduce = _____
6. plentiful = _____
7. pollution = _____
8. scarce = _____
9. global = _____

G. Find 10 words from the word list on the kite. Write them.

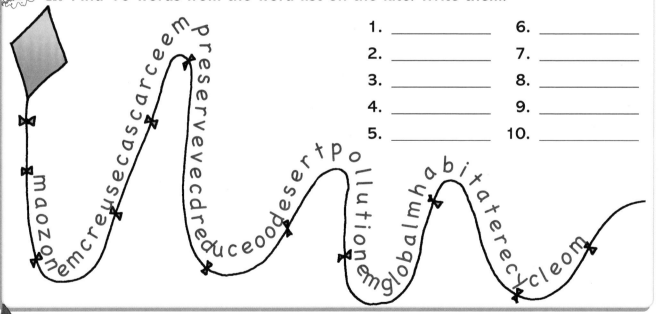

1. _____
2. _____
3. _____
4. _____
5. _____
6. _____
7. _____
8. _____
9. _____
10. _____

H. Match the letters. Write the words.

preser	al	1. _____
glob	ce	2. _____
redu	al	3. _____
scar	ful	4. _____
natur	ce	5. _____
plenti	ve	6. _____

habit	ion	7. _____
oz	use	8. _____
recy	ert	9. _____
des	one	10. _____
re	at	11. _____
pollut	cle	12. _____

Commonly Misspelled Words

Word List

❶		❷		❸		❹	
vision	opportunity	restaurant	permanent	hypocrite	insurance	irrelevant	performance
omitted	immediately	experience	intelligence	definition	camouflage	medicine	mischievous

A. Write the missing letters.

1. v __ __ ion
2. omi __ __ ed
3. opp __ __ tunity
4. i __ __ ediately

5. rest __ __ __ ant
6. exper __ __ nce
7. perm __ __ ent
8. int __ __ ligence

9. h __ __ ocrite
10. defin __ __ ion
11. insur __ __ ce
12. cam __ __ flage

13. ir __ elev __ nt
14. med __ __ ine
15. perf __ rmance
16. mischie __ __ us

B. Unscramble these words. Write them. Find them in the wordsearch.

1. nieecrexep _____
2. famoucagel _____
3. tserraautn _____
4. tomedit _____
5. nameentpr _____
6. nivsio _____
7. cpyohiter _____
8. cidemnie _____
9. vanrireelt _____
10. surenican _____

```
i  c  a  m  o  u  f  l  a  g  e  r
n  s  a  p  m  v  i  s  i  o  n  e
s  e  q  d  i  t  x  e  d  r  m  s
u  c  w  a  t  o  h  x  z  j  d  t
r  w  p  j  t  c  b  p  d  h  w  a
a  x  v  b  e  x  n  e  r  x  x  u
n  e  c  a  d  p  y  r  y  x  g  r
c  x  k  b  m  c  b  i  l  b  x  a
e  p  e  r  m  a  n  e  n  t  v  n
v  m  e  d  i  c  i  n  e  j  t  t
h  c  m  h  y  p  o  c  r  i  t  e
x  k  i  r  r  e  l  e  v  a  n  t
```

C. Write 10 words from the word list using these letters. You can use a letter more than once.

p e d x r m u l a n i s v t c o f y

1. _____
2. _____
3. _____
4. _____
5. _____
6. _____
7. _____
8. _____
9. _____
10. _____

D. Make 3 small words from each word below. You can mix up the letters.

1. insurance
2. permanent
3. restaurant
4. experience
5. camouflage

case ____ | ____ | ____ | ____ | ____
____ | ____ | ____ | ____ | ____
____ | ____ | ____ | ____ | ____

E. Crossword.

Across

1. It comes from a French word which means 'to disguise'.
6. Presenting entertainment.
8. Left out!
9. Sight or something you see in your mind.

Down

2. A chance.
3. Acquired skill or knowledge.
4. Opposite to temporary.
5. Travel and health are types of it.
7. You take it when you are ill.

F. ✗ the 8 incorrect spellings. Write them correctly.

1. experience ☐	9. opportunity ☐	_____	
2. ommited ☐	10. imediately ☐	_____	
3. intelligence ☐	11. restraunt ☐	_____	
4. vision ☐	12. hypocrit ☐	_____	
5. insurance ☐	13. mischievous ☐	_____	
6. permenent ☐	14. definition ☐	_____	
7. performance ☐	15. medecine ☐	_____	
8. camuflage ☐	16. irelevant ☐	_____	

G. Write the missing words. Use the word list.

1. _____ should be kept out of reach of young children.
2. The orchestra gave an outstanding _____.
3. The _____ of a decade is ten years.
4. Mahatma Gandhi was a leader with _____.
5. Many animals use _____ for protection.
6. 'Look at me,' said the little girl with a _____ grin.
7. He got a _____ job after a successful trial.
8. Our house _____ didn't cover bicycle theft.
9. The _____ did exactly the opposite to what he'd promised.
10. The detective thought that the clues were totally _____.

Word List

❶		❷		❸		❹	
riddle	scribble	obstacle	valuable	available	sensible	terrible	struggle
middle	miracle	portable	reliable	invisible	possible	horrible	tremble

A. Write the missing letters.

1. ri __ __ le
2. __ __ dd __ __
3. scr __ bb __ __
4. __ __ __ acl __

5. obs __ __ __ le
6. __ __ __ tabl __
7. val __ __ __ le
8. __ __ __ iabl __

9. __ __ ailab __ __
10. __ __ visi __ le
11. sen __ __ __ le
12. __ __ ss __ __ le

13. __ __ rr __ __ le
14. ho __ __ ibl __
15. str __ gg __ __
16. __ __ emb __ __

B. Make 3 small words from each word below. You can mix up the letters.

1. miracle	2. scribble	3. sensible	4. struggle	5. tremble
<u>claim</u>	_____	_____	_____	_____
_____	_____	_____	_____	_____
_____	_____	_____	_____	_____

C. Crossword.

Across

2. Puzzle.
5. An incredible outcome.
7. Can't be seen.
8. Something to be overcome.
9. Awful.

Down

1. Shake.
3. Writing that makes no sense.
4. In between two things.
6. A person or object that won't let you down.

D. Remove a letter (or letters) to make a new word.

1. mi~~dd~~le = <u>mile</u>
2. scribble = _____
3. portable = _____
4. obstacle = _____
5. possible = _____
6. invisible = _____
7. available = _____
8. horrible = _____
9. tremble = _____

E. Write the missing words. Use the word list.

1. The earthquake was a very minor one but I felt the ground _____.
2. My baby brother tried to _____ all over my homework.
3. My friend told me a _____ but I couldn't figure it out.
4. I won the _____ race at our sport's day.
5. A laptop computer is one that is _____.
6. Our neighbour asked if I was _____ to walk her dog.
7. I only began to _____ towards the end of the race.
8. My grandad lost his watch which was very _____.
9. I missed the train but by some _____ another one appeared immediately.
10. I have one older sister and one younger sister so I am in the _____.

F. Unscramble these words. Write them. Find them in the wordsearch.

1. lruesgtg   _____
2. erbtierl   _____
3. eorilrhb   _____
4. erebmlt   _____
5. psielsob   _____
6. eivsilinb   _____
7. iarlcme   _____
8. eaulvalb   _____
9. lavbilaea   _____
10. leblirae   _____

l	t	i	s	f	f	z	s	d	x	h	a
i	h	h	o	r	r	i	b	l	e	w	v
v	s	t	r	u	g	g	l	e	t	o	a
t	n	y	v	w	w	q	r	h	r	t	l
b	n	i	e	n	v	c	f	e	e	e	u
m	i	r	a	c	l	e	e	w	m	r	a
q	u	h	x	y	x	x	v	j	b	r	b
i	n	v	i	s	i	b	l	e	l	i	l
a	v	a	i	l	a	b	l	e	e	b	e
b	b	t	i	p	o	s	s	i	b	l	e
r	e	l	i	a	b	l	e	p	y	e	l
m	g	a	j	p	p	v	r	k	x	w	o

G. Write the word list in alphabetical order.

1. available   5. _____   9. _____   13. _____
2. _____   6. _____   10. _____   14. _____
3. _____   7. _____   11. _____   15. _____
4. _____   8. _____   12. _____   16. valuable

H. Match the letters. Write the words.

obst	ible	1. _____		trem	able	7. _____
val	ddle	2. _____		mir	ibble	8. _____
str	uable	3. _____		invis	ble	9. _____
poss	acle	4. _____		scr	acle	10. _____
mid	uggle	5. _____		avail	able	11. _____
ri	dle	6. _____		port	ible	12. _____

Theme: Transport and Travel

Word List

conductor ❶ hovercraft	platform ❷ station	pedestrian ❸ submarine	foreign ❹ temperature
rocket ferry	porter tourist	passport language	uniform scenery

A. Write the missing letters.

1. con __ __ __ tor
2. ro __ __ __ t
3. h __ __ __ __ rcraft
4. fe __ __ y

5. pl __ __ __ orm
6. p __ __ t __ __
7. st __ __ ion
8. t __ __ rist

9. p __ __ __ strian
10. pa __ __ port
11. sub __ __ __ ine
12. lang __ __ ge

13. for __ __ __ n
14. un __ __ orm
15. temperatu __ __
16. sc __ __ __ ry

B. Crossword.

Across

3. You need it to travel abroad.
5. A metal tube used to launch a spacecraft.
7. Someone who carries your luggage.
8. Someone who checks your ticket.

Down

1. A place where trains stop on a railway line.
2. Outside your country.
4. They sat on the mountaintop and admired the __ __ __ __ __ __ __.
6. A visitor to an area.

C. Write the word list in alphabetical order.

1. <u>conductor</u>
2. _____
3. _____
4. _____

5. _____
6. _____
7. _____
8. _____

9. _____
10. _____
11. _____
12. _____

13. _____
14. _____
15. _____
16. <u>uniform</u>

D. Write a word from the word list that contains these letters.

1. es _____
2. ei _____
3. et _____

4. er _____
5. or _____
6. ou _____

7. ua _____
8. at _____
9. ft _____

E. Unscramble these words. Write them. Find them in the wordsearch.

1. eifrong   _____
2. routsit   _____
3. ctekro   _____
4. finroum   _____
5. tastnio   _____
6. ggauenla   _____
7. docncurot   _____
8. tropre   _____
9. refyr   _____
10. trdepesina   _____

```
u u t g d c c j i p z s
f b l n f o a z n o y g
r d p i t n a s y r t x
o u k z p d f a r t x o
c h y r n u o v f e k g
k b i h v c v j o r e c
e l q v y t o u r i s t
t u n i f o r m e p w f
q w n l k r c o i x b e
r n l a n g u a g e r r
s t a t i o n i n h w r
x p e d e s t r i a n y
```

F. Remove a letter (or letters) to make a new word.

1. ~~su~~b~~ma~~rine = <u>mine</u>
2. conductor = _____
3. rocket = _____
4. pedestrian = _____
5. platform = _____
6. scenery = _____
7. hovercraft = _____
8. foreign = _____
9. language = _____

G. Find 10 words from the word list on the kite. Write them.

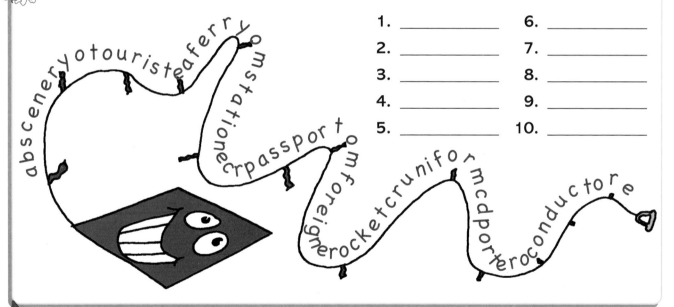

1. _____   6. _____
2. _____   7. _____
3. _____   8. _____
4. _____   9. _____
5. _____   10. _____

H. Match the letters. Write the words.

unifo	gn	1. _____	scene	er	7. _____
forei	ion	2. _____	conduct	ge	8. _____
rock	ure	3. _____	langua	ist	9. _____
pedestr	rm	4. _____	port	ry	10. _____
temperat	ian	5. _____	fer	or	11. _____
stat	et	6. _____	tour	ry	12. _____

Word List

❶	❷	❸	❹
twice entice	notice service	practice reduce	replace surface
price device	police justice	advice produce	disgrace introduce

A. Write the missing letters.

1. tw __ __ __ __

2. __ __ ice

3. en __ __ ce

4. __ __ vi __ __

5. not __ __ __

6. __ __ __ ice

7. serv __ __ __

8. __ __ __ __ ice

9. pr __ __ __ ice

10. __ __ vi __ __

11. red __ __ __

12. __ __ __ __ __ uce

13. re __ __ ace

14. __ __ __ grac __

15. __ __ __ __ fac __

16. int __ __ __ uce

B. Make 3 small words from each word below. You can mix up the letters.

1. device   2. notice   3. reduce   4. produce   5. surface

dive _____   _____   _____   _____   _____

_____   _____   _____   _____   _____

_____   _____   _____   _____   _____

C. Crossword.

Across

2. Shameful outcome.

7. Observe.

8. Doing work for someone.

9. Make smaller.

Down

1. Assistance or guidance.

3. The top layer.

4. The cost of an item.

5. Two times.

6. They are responsible for keeping law and order.

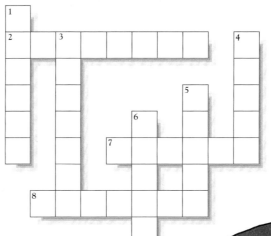

D. Remove a letter (or letters) to make a new word.

1. entice = nice

2. device = _____

3. practice = _____

4. disgrace = _____

5. surface = _____

6. advice = _____

7. introduce = _____

8. replace = _____

9. notice = _____

E. Write the missing words. Use the word list.

1. I put out bird seed to _____ the robin into the garden.
2. I am going to have to _____ my old football boots.
3. The amount of litter on the street was a _____.
4. The shop will _____ its prices for the sale.
5. I had a little _____ for making milkshakes.
6. The pond skater travels on the _____ of the pond.
7. I am going to _____ the new girl to all my friends.
8. My tomato plant will _____ about twenty tomatoes.
9. I lost the tennis match as I was out of _____.
10. After the court case the man felt that _____ had been done.

F. Unscramble these words. Write them. Find them in the wordsearch.

1. icratpce _____ _____
2. edcaiv _____
3. encrtouid _____
4. dueocrp _____
5. rfsaeuc _____
6. eecvisr _____
7. irdcgesa _____
8. nceite _____
9. rpaelce _____
10. ejctius _____

p	d	g	a	d	v	i	c	e	q	d	p
s	d	i	n	t	r	o	d	u	c	e	r
c	u	x	p	r	o	d	u	c	e	q	a
q	d	r	o	s	p	v	t	j	g	z	c
n	n	t	f	y	j	w	s	l	h	d	t
e	e	t	a	a	h	a	w	u	e	s	i
d	r	w	d	e	c	l	z	l	i	p	c
d	r	s	e	q	m	e	g	b	d	l	e
t	d	i	s	g	r	a	c	e	a	m	m
j	u	s	t	i	c	e	n	t	i	c	e
v	x	j	s	e	r	v	i	c	e	x	u
r	e	p	l	a	c	e	d	j	o	g	m

G. Write the word list in alphabetical order.

1. advice
2. _____
3. _____
4. _____
5. _____
6. _____
7. _____
8. _____
9. _____
10. _____
11. _____
12. _____
13. _____
14. _____
15. _____
16. twice

H. Match the letters. Write the words.

dis	ice	1. _____
rep	uce	2. _____
ser	lace	3. _____
just	grace	4. _____
po	vice	5. _____
red	lice	6. _____

introd	face	7. _____
dev	ctice	8. _____
sur	uce	9. _____
pra	duce	10. _____
pro	vice	11. _____
ad	ice	12. _____

Word List

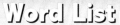

mystery ❶ grocery	brewery ❷ flowery	jewellery ❸ machinery	flattery ❹ monastery
surgery nursery	bribery showery	cemetery discovery	slippery stationery

A. Write the missing letters.

1. my __ __ ery
2. __ __ __ ger __
3. gr __ __ er __
4. __ __ __ ser __

5. br __ __ ery
6. __ __ __ ib __ __ y
7. __ __ owe __ __ __
8. sh __ __ er __

9. je __ __ ller __
10. __ __ met __ ry
11. mach __ __ ery
12. discov __ __ y

13. fla __ __ er __
14. __ __ __ i __ pery
15. mon __ __ tery
16. __ __ ation __ ry

B. Make 3 small words from each word below. You can mix up the letters.

1. mystery   2. nursery   3. brewery   4. showery   5. surgery

stem ____   _____   _____   _____   _____

_____   _____   _____   _____   _____

_____   _____   _____   _____   _____

C. Crossword.

Across

2. Full of flowers.
6. Lots of light rain.
7. A place where beer is made.
8. A medical procedure.

Down

1. A building where monks live.
2. Insincere praise.
3. Making someone act in your interest.
4. A burial ground.
5. A situation that has no explanation.

D. Remove a letter (or letters) to make a new word.

1. flattery = fly
2. slippery = _____
3. discovery = _____

4. flowery = _____
5. jewellery = _____
6. cemetery = _____

7. surgery = _____
8. mystery = _____
9. bribery = _____

E. Write the missing words. Use the word list.

1. I was at a show that had different farm _____ on display.
2. After the heavy rain the roads were very _____.
3. My great grandfather is buried in our local _____.
4. My cousin broke her arm and needed _____.
5. _____ weather has been forecast for the next few days.
6. The only _____ I have is a bracelet and a ring.
7. The detectives failed to solve the _____.
8. I walked to our local _____ shop to get some dog food.
9. I'm going to buy some _____ so I can write to my grandmother.
10. My younger sister goes to a _____ from 9 o'clock to midday.

F. Unscramble these words. Write them. Find them in the wordsearch.

1. rftealty _____
2. yechnmiar _____
3. ricoedvsy _____
4. lereyjlwe _____
5. rgesruy _____
6. yonemsatr _____
7. yleipspr _____
8. netraosity _____
9. yetmecer _____
10. yrsemyt _____

s	l	i	p	p	c	r	y	m	r	j	s
c	e	m	e	t	e	r	y	y	k	u	n
f	l	a	t	t	e	r	y	s	i	d	i
l	s	h	n	c	y	k	a	t	l	i	j
s	w	m	g	y	y	e	t	e	t	s	e
s	t	a	t	i	o	n	e	r	y	c	w
k	o	k	b	w	e	f	h	y	t	o	e
m	o	n	a	s	t	e	r	y	z	v	l
s	u	r	g	e	r	y	p	c	q	e	l
o	q	s	s	n	a	v	d	c	k	r	e
p	s	x	v	r	a	i	v	o	l	y	r
m	a	c	h	i	n	e	r	y	c	x	y

G. Write the word list in alphabetical order.

1. _brewery_   5. _____   9. _____   13. _____
2. _____   6. _____   10. _____   14. _____
3. _____   7. _____   11. _____   15. _____
4. _____   8. _____   12. _____   16. _surgery_

H. Match the letters. Write the words.

jewel	ry	1. _____		flat	ery	7. _____
cem	ery	2. _____		disco	y	8. _____
machine	etery	3. _____		brew	tery	9. _____
mon	lery	4. _____		shower	pery	10. _____
flo	astery	5. _____		slip	bery	11. _____
station	wery	6. _____		bri	very	12. _____

UNIT 16

Word List

Latvia	① Netherlands	Estonia	② Romania	Luxembourg	③ Egypt	Switzerland	④ Russia
Lithuania	Hungary	Cyprus	Brazil	Poland	Canada	Australia	Nigeria

A. Write the missing letters.

1. Lat __ __ __
2. Lithu __ __ ia
3. Net __ __ rlands
4. Hun __ __ ry

5. Es __ __ __ ia
6. C __ __ rus
7. R __ __ __ nia
8. Br __ __ il

9. Luxemb __ __ rg
10. P __ __ and
11. E __ __ __ __ t
12. C __ n __ da

13. Swi __ __ erland
14. A __ __ trali __
15. Russ __ __
16. Nig __ __ ia

B. Crossword. The clues are the capital cities of these countries. Name the countries.

Across

1. Vilnius.
5. Cairo.
7. Budapest.
8. Ottawa
9. Moscow.

Down

1. Riga.
2. Abuja.
3. Canberra.
4. Tallinn.
6. Nicosia.

Crossword grid: 1 across spelled L I T H U A N I A

C. Write the word list in alphabetical order.

1. _____
2. _____
3. _____
4. _____

5. _____
6. _____
7. _____
8. _____

9. _____
10. _____
11. _____
12. _____

13. _____
14. _____
15. _____
16. _____

D. Write a word from the word list that contains these letters.

1. ia _____
2. ss _____
3. er _____

4. ua _____
5. an _____
6. ru _____

7. ar _____
8. ge _____
9. li _____

Unscramble these words. Write them. Find them in the wordsearch.

1. NPDOLA _____
2. PYSUCR _____
3. SIASUR _____
4. AGNHUYR _____
5. YTPGE _____
6. NAIAHULIT _____
7. EIAGINR _____
8. NAIRMOA _____
9. AAANCD _____
10. SRALAUTAI _____

P	O	L	A	N	D	C	Y	P	R	U	S
E	S	U	D	Z	D	A	C	K	L	O	F
I	N	T	H	D	P	N	M	H	I	W	D
K	J	V	S	R	Q	A	K	U	T	Q	C
J	B	O	Z	U	H	D	E	I	H	X	F
C	C	B	B	S	U	A	R	Q	U	P	D
N	Z	N	U	S	I	J	T	F	A	L	T
G	Z	G	W	I	R	O	M	A	N	I	A
H	U	N	G	A	R	Y	B	I	I	E	K
N	I	G	E	R	I	A	G	K	A	H	T
K	P	L	A	U	S	T	R	A	L	I	A
E	G	Y	P	T	G	M	U	I	K	Z	O

F. **Remove a letter (or letters) to make a new word.**

1. ~~Es~~toni~~a~~ = _ton_____   4. Hungary = _____   7. Lithuania = _____
2. Romania = _____   5. Canada = _____   8. Latvia = _____
3. Poland = _____   6. Australia = _____   9. Russia = _____

G. **Find 10 words from the word list on the kite. Write them.**

1. _____   6. _____
2. _____   7. _____
3. _____   8. _____
4. _____   9. _____
5. _____   10. _____

H. **Match the letters. Write the words.**

Lat	rg	1. _____	Egy	il	7. _____
Cypr	ia	2. _____	Pola	ary	8. _____
Can	via	3. _____	Braz	nia	9. _____
Esto	us	4. _____	Hung	pt	10. _____
Austral	nia	5. _____	Russ	nd	11. _____
Luxembou	ada	6. _____	Lithua	ia	12. _____

Word List

❶		❷		❸		❹	
union	million	billion	companion	scorpion	junior	inferior	exterior
onion	opinion	champion	accordion	stallion	senior	superior	interior

A. Write the missing letters.

1. un __ __ __
2. __ __ ion
3. mi __ __ ion
4. __ __ in __ __ __

5. bi __ __ ion
6. __ __ ampi __ __
7. __ __ __ panion
8. a __ __ ordio __

9. sc __ __ __ ion
10. __ __ alli __ __
11. jun __ __ __
12. __ __ ni __ __

13. inf __ __ ior
14. __ __ __ __ erio __
15. ext __ __ ior
16. __ __ __ __ erio __

B. Make 3 small words from each word below. You can mix up the letters.

1. million   2. union   3. opinion   4. billion   5. superior

<u>oil</u> ___ ___ ___ ___ ___

___ ___ ___ ___ ___

___ ___ ___ ___ ___

C. Crossword.

Across

5. A vegetable.
6. Opposite to exterior.
7. Older.
8. It has pincers and a poisonous sting.

Down

1. Joining together.
2. A musical instrument.
3. Opposite to superior.
4. Younger.

D. Remove a letter (or letters) to make a new word.

1. ~~billion~~ = <u>bin</u>
2. opinion = _____
3. champion = _____
4. scorpion = _____
5. accordion = _____
6. companion = _____
7. superior = _____
8. stallion = _____
9. million = _____

Write the missing words. Use the word list.

1. I started learning how to play the _____ at the age of nine.

2. Whenever I chop an _____ I start to cry!

3. The black _____ leaped over the high fence.

4. My younger sister is in the _____ school.

5. My new bicycle is far _____ to my old one.

6. I have only ever seen a _____ at the zoo.

7. I'd like to train to be an _____ designer.

8. My neighbour won a _____ euro in the Lottery.

9. It looked as if there were at least a _____ stars in the sky.

10. The outside of the house is being painted using _____ paint.

F. **Unscramble these words. Write them. Find them in the wordsearch.**

1. ocnrispo ___ _____ ___

2. ltiaosln _____

3. nhaocimp _____

4. oueisrpr _____

5. rxereito _____

6. ncriadoco _____

7. inroietr _____

8. inerirfo _____

9. iopncanmo _____

10. ipniono _____

t	d	t	s	u	p	e	r	i	o	r	i
v	y	t	f	f	d	t	q	r	e	e	n
i	n	f	e	r	i	o	r	j	q	l	t
o	a	h	b	e	b	u	h	m	y	y	e
q	s	c	o	r	p	i	o	n	s	s	r
n	f	z	r	p	a	c	u	v	m	t	i
x	m	h	m	m	i	n	r	n	e	a	o
a	n	f	y	j	h	n	f	t	d	l	r
g	a	c	c	o	r	d	i	o	n	l	a
c	h	a	m	p	i	o	n	o	f	i	y
e	x	t	e	r	i	o	r	y	n	o	v
r	b	c	o	m	p	a	n	i	o	n	w

G. **Write the word list in alphabetical order.**

1. _accordion_   5. _____   9. _____   13. _____

2. _____   6. _____   10. _____   14. _____

3. _____   7. _____   11. _____   15. _____

4. _____   8. _____   12. _____   16. _union_

H. **Match the letters. Write the words.**

mill	nior	1. _____		inf	ior	7. _____
cham	erior	2. _____		stal	on	8. _____
comp	ion	3. _____		jun	erior	9. _____
se	anion	4. _____		scor	lion	10. _____
ext	ior	5. _____		accord	pion	11. _____
super	pion	6. _____		uni	ion	12. _____

Commonly Misspelled Words

Word List

❶		❷		❸		❹	
hygiene	valuable	nuisance	necessary	proceed	ignorance	physical	government
column	success	occasion	loneliness	disease	knowledge	generally	introduce

A. Write the missing letters.

1. hyg __ __ ne
2. col __ __ __
3. val __ __ b __ __ __
4. su __ __ e __ s

5. n __ __ s __ nce
6. o __ __ asion
7. nece __ __ ar __
8. lon __ __ iness

9. p __ __ c __ ed
10. dis __ __ se
11. ig __ __ __ ance
12. kno __ le __ ge

13. p __ __ sic __ l
14. gen __ __ ally
15. gover __ ment
16. in __ __ __ duce

B. Unscramble these words. Write them. Find them in the wordsearch.

1. llyeearng   _____
2. lbauelva   _____
3. ccoianos   _____
4. ccssseu   _____
5. isseead   _____
6. ineeghy   _____
7. cislayph   _____
8. scenainu   _____
9. nemntevorg   _____
10. mcnluo   _____

```
v h w g q i z u f b k x
a u s o j y r q j r g h
l c a v c o l u m n h a
u q l e d i s e a s e m
a l s r h y g i e n e c
b v u n a d p r e e r w
l h c m h j l s z v f c
e s c e p h y s i c a l
h g e n e r a l l y d q
c t s t n u i s a n c e
l z s b u q j b m u p n
o c c a s i o n a e f a
```

C. Write 10 words from the word list using these letters. You can use a letter more than once.

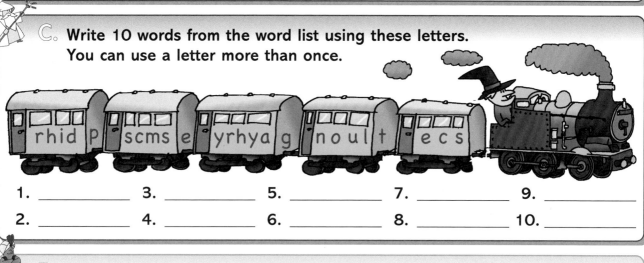

r h i d P   scms e   yrhya g   n o u l t   e c s

1. _____
2. _____
3. _____
4. _____
5. _____
6. _____
7. _____
8. _____
9. _____
10. _____

D. Make 3 small words from each word below. You can mix up the letters.

1. knowledge   2. introduce   3. loneliness   4. government   5. valuable

<u>lend</u> _____ _____ _____ _____

_____ _____ _____ _____ _____

_____ _____ _____ _____ _____

E. Crossword.

Across

5. Usually.

7. Required in order to be done.

Down

1. Health and

＿ ＿ ＿ ＿ ＿ ＿ ＿.

2. It is very important to you.

3. ＿ ＿ ＿ ＿ ＿ ＿ ＿ ＿ ＿ and

political maps.

4. Move on!

6. Someone or something

that causes trouble.

It is forbidden to eat this notice.

F. ✗ the 8 incorrect spellings. Write them correctly.

1. ignorence	☐	9. necessery	☐
2. colum	☐	10. proceed	☐
3. physical	☐	11. hygeine	☐
4. loneliness	☐	12. disease	☐
5. success	☐	13. nuisance	☐
6. generally	☐	14. knoledge	☐
7. ocassion	☐	15. interoduce	☐
8. government	☐	16. valuble	☐

_____

_____

_____

_____

_____

_____

_____

_____

G. Write the missing words. Use the word list.

1. '＿＿＿＿＿ Education is my favourite subject.'

2. My grandmother's 80th birthday was a special ＿＿＿＿＿.

3. '＿＿＿＿＿ with caution,' warned the team leader.

4. There's an old saying: '＿＿＿＿＿ is bliss'.

5. A new ＿＿＿＿＿ was formed after the election.

6. Some people love reading the gossip ＿＿＿＿＿ in the

newspaper.

7. They say that a little ＿＿＿＿＿ is a dangerous thing!

8. They were delighted that the show was such a ＿＿＿＿＿.

9. Many people who live alone suffer from ＿＿＿＿＿.

10. The restaurant was closed down because of poor ＿＿＿＿＿.

UNIT 19

Word List

❶		❷		❸		❹	
editor	mechanic	engineer	scientist	chemist	secretary	electrician	surgeon
lawyer	professor	optician	athlete	librarian	journalist	jockey	musician

A. Write the missing letters.

1. edit __ __
2. law __ __ r
3. me __ __ ani __
4. prof __ __ __ or
5. engin __ __ r
6. o __ __ ic __ an
7. sc __ __ ntist
8. a __ __ __ ete
9. ch __ __ __ st
10. lib __ __ __ ian
11. sec __ __ __ ary
12. jo __ __ __ alist
13. el __ __ __ rician
14. j __ __ __ ey
15. sur __ __ __ n
16. mus __ __ ian

B. Crossword.

Across

3. A person who competes at sport.
6. He/she tests your eyesight.
7. Works in a theatre! Not an actor!
8. A person who decides on the content of a book, newspaper etc.
9. Marie Curie was a famous one.

Down

1. An expert on law.
2. Someone who writes for a newspaper.
4. A person who designs and builds engines.
5. A person who studies science.

C. Write the word list in alphabetical order.

1. athlete
2. _____
3. _____
4. _____
5. _____
6. _____
7. _____
8. _____
9. _____
10. _____
11. _____
12. _____
13. _____
14. _____
15. _____
16. surgeon

D. Write a word from the word list that contains these letters.

1. ee _____
   ian _____
   er _____
4. ou _____
5. ie _____
6. ar _____
7. ur _____
8. or _____
9. at _____

40

E. Unscramble these words. Write them. Find them in the wordsearch.

1. canitipo _____
2. mehtics _____
3. cichemna _____
4. oneugrs _____
5. taeelht _____
6. niabarril _____
7. roteid _____
8. rsetecrya _____
9. ernignee _____
10. cmiusnai _____

```
a e d i t o r p x e m h
t m h m a p o c m n u u
h r m t g t h c l g s h
l o d f m i v h b i i g
e d z r r c y e a n c s
t z l g w i v m p e i u
e m e c h a n i c e a r
n w d f e n v s u r n g
c h z a y w s t p d z e
d h u r k f j x u c h o
l i b r a r i a n i j n
g z s e c r e t a r y p
```

F. Remove a letter (or letters) to make a new word.

1. me~~ch~~ani~~c~~ = mean_____
2. professor = _____
3. athlete = _____
4. librarian = _____
5. engineer = _____
6. journalist = _____
7. optician = _____
8. scientist = _____
9. electrician = _____

G. Find 10 words from the word list on the kite. Write them.

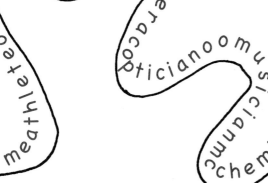
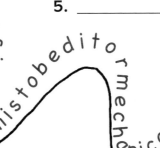
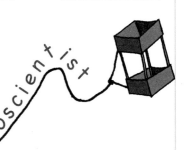

1. _____
2. _____
3. _____
4. _____
5. _____
6. _____
7. _____
8. _____
9. _____
10. _____

H. Match the letters. Write the words.

athl	ian	1. _____	
engin	er	2. _____	
librar	eon	3. _____	
lawy	or	4. _____	
surg	ete	5. _____	
profess	eer	6. _____	

optic	or	7. _____	
jock	ist	8. _____	
secret	ic	9. _____	
edit	ey	10. _____	
scient	ian	11. _____	
mechan	ary	12. _____	

uNIT 20

Word List

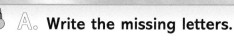

❶		❷		❸		❹	
special	crucial	martial	partial	especially	torrential	official	confidential
social	initial	facial	financial	essential	impartial	artificial	influential

A. Write the missing letters.

1. sp __ __ ial
2. s __ __ __ a __
3. cr __ __ ial
4. __ __ it __ __ __
5. ma __ __ ial
6. __ __ __ ial
7. __ __ rt __ __ __ __
8. fin __ __ __ ial
9. espe __ ial __ y
10. e __ __ enti __ l
11. torrenti __ __
12. imp __ __ __ ial
13. o __ __ ici __ __
14. __ __ __ __ ifi __ ial
15. confide __ __ ial
16. influent __ __ __ __

B. Make 3 small words from each word below. You can mix up the letters.

1. special
   <u>cape</u>
   _____
   _____

2. partial
   _____
   _____
   _____

3. torrential
   _____
   _____
   _____

4. especially
   _____
   _____
   _____

5. confidential
   _____
   _____
   _____

C. Crossword.

Across
5. The first.
6. In favour of.
7. Vital.
8. Exceptional.
9. Particularly.

Down
1. Relating to money matters.
2. __ __ __ __ __ __ __ __ __ arts.
3. Having an effect on.
4. Not taking sides.

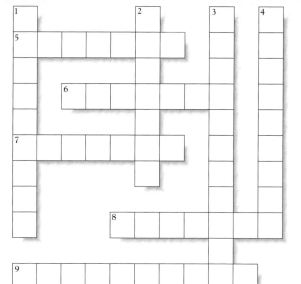

D. Remove a letter (or letters) to make a new word.

1. ~~martial~~ = <u>art</u>
2. essential = _____
3. especially = _____
4. torrential = _____
5. influential = _____
6. official = _____
7. special = _____
8. social = _____
9. impartial = _____

E. Write the missing words. Use the word list.

1. The label on the tin of soup said it had no _____ ingredients.
2. My _____ impression of my new school was very positive.
3. I wrote private and _____ on the cover of my diary.
4. We had a thunderstorm followed by _____ rain.
5. Our dog has only _____ sight in one eye.
6. We felt that the judgement was fair and _____.
7. It is ____ _____ to wear a seat belt in a car.
8. I love the weekends, _____ Saturdays.
9. I found a lost kitten but refused to take the _____ reward.
10. I left out an _____ ingredient of the recipe and the cake flopped.

F. Unscramble these words. Write them. Find them in the wordsearch.

1. aariptl   _____
2. loaritetrn   _____
3. lificofa   _____
4. alimtra   _____
5. arclciu   _____
6. acrlfiaiti   _____
7. afialc   _____
8. lamrtiapi   _____
9. ylseceipal _____
10. ailncfani   _____

a	r	t	i	f	i	c	i	a	l	f	k
c	r	u	c	i	a	l	a	t	j	a	m
m	a	r	t	i	a	l	v	j	k	c	g
t	e	u	e	m	t	n	m	i	p	i	t
p	a	c	p	a	r	t	i	a	l	a	o
f	i	n	a	n	c	i	a	l	k	l	f
i	e	s	p	e	c	i	a	l	l	y	f
z	h	h	x	r	b	y	y	k	i	i	i
w	m	f	u	r	m	m	n	f	m	n	c
x	i	i	a	d	z	i	m	c	y	t	i
i	m	p	a	r	t	i	a	l	e	e	a
t	o	r	r	e	n	t	i	a	l	q	l

G. Write the word list in alphabetical order.

1. <u>artificial</u>
2. _____
3. _____
4. _____
5. _____
6. _____
7. _____
8. _____
9. _____
10. _____
11. _____
12. _____
13. _____
14. _____
15. _____
16. <u>torrential</u>

H. Match the letters. Write the words.

essen	ially	1. _____
part	icial	2. _____
espec	tial	3. _____
off	ential	4. _____
torr	cial	5. _____
spe	ial	6. _____

impart	tial	7. _____
confid	icial	8. _____
infl	cial	9. _____
mar	uential	10. _____
artif	ial	11. _____
finan	ential	12. _____

uNIT 21

Word List

❶	❷	❸	❹
distant ignorant	pleasant assistant	silent excellent	enjoyment violent
brilliant servant	elephant extravagant	accident confident	student experiment

A. Write the missing letters.

1. di __ __ ant
2. __ __ illi __ __ t
3. ig __ __ __ ant
4. __ __ rv __ __ __ __

5. pl __ __ __ ant
6. __ __ epha __ __
7. a __ __ istan __
8. ex __ __ avagant

9. sil __ __ __ __
10. __ cc __ __ ent
11. ex __ __ llen __
12. con __ __ __ ent

13. en __ __ yment
14. __ __ ude __ __
15. __ __ ole __ __
16. ex __ __ riment

B. Make 3 small words from each word below. You can mix up the letters.

1. distant
   <u>said</u>
   _____
   _____

2. servant
   _____
   _____
   _____

3. silent
   _____
   _____
   _____

4. pleasant
   _____
   _____
   _____

5. violent
   _____
   _____
   _____

C. Crossword.

Across

1. There is an Indian and an African one.
4. Pupil.
7. Rude.
8. Self-assured.

Down

2. Nice.
3. Superb.
4. Quiet.
5. An unfortunate incident.
6. A person who sees to the needs of others.

D. Remove a letter (or letters) to make a new word.

1. si~~l~~ent = <u>sent</u>
2. experiment = _____
3. confident = _____
4. brilliant = _____
5. pleasant = _____
6. ignorant = _____

E. Write the missing words. Use the word list.

1. I was _____ that we could win the match.

2. My first day at school is only a _____ memory.

3. We conducted our first _____ in the science laboratory.

4. The fireworks display was _____.

5. The cloudy day didn't spoil our _____ of the picnic.

6. My older sister is a first year _____ at university.

7. The new boy was _____ at maths.

8. The king asked his _____ to bring him his crown.

9. My sister has a sore throat and for once she was _____.

10. The African _____ is much bigger than the Indian one.

F. Unscramble these words. Write them. Find them in the wordsearch.

1. otilnve   _____

2. xmrietenpe _____

3. tstisaasn   _____

4. tiandts   _____

5. nlehepat   _____

6. tgonrian   _____

7. eelcelnxt   _____

8. nialbilrt   _____

9. tensdut   _____

10. apenstal   _____

n	p	l	e	a	s	a	n	t	r	v	j
r	q	b	y	b	p	t	l	p	i	i	e
e	z	s	s	g	g	r	e	p	c	o	s
t	a	r	n	g	q	n	s	u	k	l	i
e	x	c	e	l	l	e	n	t	s	e	g
f	a	s	s	i	s	t	a	n	t	n	n
d	i	s	t	a	n	t	b	m	a	t	o
p	t	r	n	w	j	o	u	p	a	q	r
z	w	c	m	k	e	n	a	d	e	s	a
e	l	e	p	h	a	n	t	f	e	x	n
b	r	i	l	l	i	a	n	t	g	n	t
e	x	p	e	r	i	m	e	n	t	j	t

G. Write the word list in alphabetical order.

1. accident   5. _____   9. _____   13. _____

2. _____   6. _____   10. _____   14. _____

3. _____   7. _____   11. _____   15. _____

4. _____   8. _____   12. _____   16. violent

H. Match the letters. Write the words.

dis	ent	1. _____
vio	iant	2. _____
brill	ment	3. _____
sil	tant	4. _____
plea	lent	5. _____
enjoy	sant	6. _____

exper	ant	7. _____
ele	tant	8. _____
extra	iment	9. _____
assis	phant	10. _____
stud	vagant	11. _____
ignor	ent	12. _____

45

Word List

❶		❷		❸		❹	
vertical	isosceles	area	breadth	pyramid	diagonal	parallel	equation
sphere	arc	cylinder	kilometre	protractor	decimal	capacity	symmetry

A. Write the missing letters.

1. vert __ __ al
2. s __ __ ere
3. is __ __ __ eles
4. ar __

5. ar __ __
6. c __ __ inder
7. bre __ __ th
8. kilomet __ __

9. p __ __ amid
10. protract __ __
11. d __ __ __ onal
12. d __ __ imal

13. para __ __ el
14. cap __ __ ity
15. eq __ __ tion
16. sy __ __ etr __

B. Crossword.

Across

1. This type of triangle has two equal sides.
7. Length x breadth.
8. A 3D shape seen in Egypt!
9. A part of the circumference of a circle.
10. A 3D shape that rolls.

Down

2. 8 x 3 = 24 is an __ __ __ __ __ __ __ __.
3. A 3D object shaped like a ball.
4. Opposite to horizontal.
5. Area = length x __ __ __ __ __ __ __.
6. How much something holds.

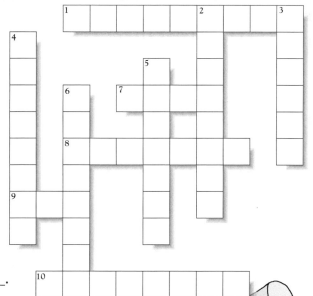

C. Write the word list in alphabetical order.

1. arc
2. _____
3. _____
4. _____

5. _____
6. _____
7. _____
8. _____

9. _____
10. _____
11. _____
12. _____

13. _____
14. _____
15. _____
16. vertical

D. Write a word from the word list that contains these letters.

1. ea _____
2. ll _____
3. al _____

4. mm _____
5. er _____
6. ia _____

7. or _____
8. ua _____
9. ra _____

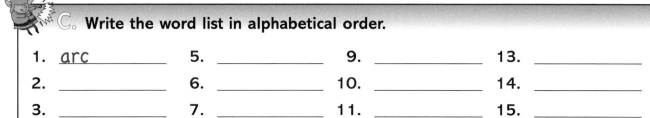

Unscramble these words. Write them. Find them in the wordsearch.

1. paciytac _____
2. elsessioc _____
3. cmlaide _____
4. daerbht _____
5. claitver _____
6. ntoiqaeu _____
7. rplllaae _____
8. esehpr _____
9. rymidap _____
10. rlcydnie _____

```
c y l i n d e r q x o n
h s u c u v u e i f d e
i y c b c j y w d h d q
f k d e c i m a l u f u
q m u a y h d e t t u a
i s o s c e l e s z z t
g r x c a p a c i t y i
q k t b r e a d t h n o
y m p y r a m i d x a n
s p h e r e p c e n d h
m g v e r t i c a l z h
p a r a l l e l x w b u
```

F. **Remove a letter (or letters) to make a new word.**

1. ~~sp~~here = <u>here</u>
2. cylinder = _____
3. protractor = _____
4. diagonal = _____
5. breadth = _____
6. parallel = _____
7. symmetry = _____
8. pyramid = _____
9. decimal = _____

G. **Find 10 words from the word list on the kite. Write them.**

mearcedecimalmnbreadthonpyramidcndreaomcapacitydtspheredbdiagonalverticalobcylinderal

1. _____   6. _____
2. _____   7. _____
3. _____   8. _____
4. _____   9. _____
5. _____   10. _____

H. **Match the letters. Write the words.**

kilomet	al	1. _____
protract	al	2. _____
equat	or	3. _____
vertic	er	4. _____
cylind	re	5. _____
decim	ion	6. _____

pyram	el	7. _____
isoscel	re	8. _____
parall	th	9. _____
sphe	al	10. _____
bread	es	11. _____
diagon	id	12. _____

Word List

❶	❷	❸	❹
handshake everybody	handmade stepladder	snowflake background	lifetime thunderstorm
daydreams footprint	wintertime fingerprint	homesick tablespoon	seashore loudspeaker

A. Write the missing letters.

1. hand __ __ ake
2. __ __ __ __ dreams
3. every __ __ __ __ y
4. foot __ __ __ __ nt
5. __ __ __ __ dmade
6. __ int __ rtime
7. stepl __ dd __ r
8. fi __ __ __ erprint
9. __ __ __ __ __ flake
10. home __ __ __ ck
11. __ __ ckground
12. tabl __ sp __ on
13. __ __ __ __ __ time
14. __ __ __ __ shore
15. thunderst __ rm
16. loudspeak __ __

B. Make 3 small words from each word below. You can mix up the letters.

1. footprint   2. homesick   3. lifetime   4. everybody   5. handshake

_trip_____   _____   _____   _____   _____

_____   _____   _____   _____   _____

_____   _____   _____   _____   _____

C. Crossword.

Across

6. A unique pattern of lines and curves.
7. A short, folding ladder.

Down

1. It has sixfold symmetry.
2. Impression left by a shoe or foot.
3. All of your life.
4. A longing for home.
5. Shaking a person's hand.

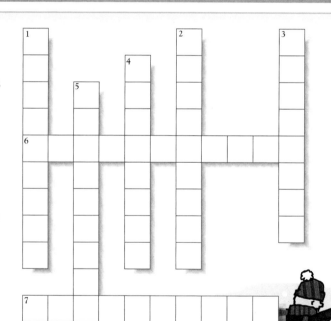

D. Remove a letter (or letters) to make a new word.

1. background = _around_
2. wintertime = _____
3. seashore = _____
4. lifetime = _____
5. snowflake = _____
6. tablespoon = _____
7. footprint = _____
8. homesick = _____
9. handmade = _____

E. Write the missing words. Use the word list.

1. I used a _____ to measure out the amount of flour required.

2. After a week at the camp I began to feel _____.

3. The man looked frail but had a very firm _____.

4. The seaweed was strewn all along the _____.

5. The thief left his _____ on the safe.

6. The flight delay was announced over the _____.

7. In _____ the trees were covered in snow.

8. The tin of paint fell off the top of the _____.

9. I have _____ about being a famous writer.

10. My aunt sent me a jewellery box that was _____ in Italy.

F. Unscramble these words. Write them. Find them in the wordsearch.

1. pnotrfoit _____

2. mieltfie _____

3. resshaoe _____

4. rdtpsleade _____

5. aadhsnhke _____

6. dbveyeroy _____

7. kmechsoi _____

8. osnaebtlpo _____

9. kowsfanle _____

10. ducgbkaron _____

s	n	o	w	f	l	a	k	e	w	r	e
h	o	m	e	s	i	c	k	t	d	y	v
s	e	a	s	h	o	r	e	a	y	f	e
g	h	l	d	j	b	n	n	b	l	o	r
t	y	e	x	h	u	g	m	l	l	o	y
s	t	e	p	l	a	d	d	e	r	t	b
c	v	b	c	l	u	m	k	s	e	p	o
e	n	r	z	x	q	v	x	p	y	r	d
l	i	f	e	t	i	m	e	o	p	i	y
q	o	b	a	c	k	g	r	o	u	n	d
l	x	e	n	k	n	y	e	n	g	t	o
h	a	n	d	s	h	a	k	e	l	v	h

G. Write the word list in alphabetical order.

1. <u>background</u>
2. _____
3. _____
4. _____
5. _____
6. _____
7. _____
8. _____
9. _____
10. _____
11. _____
12. _____
13. _____
14. _____
15. _____
16. <u>wintertime</u>

H. Match the letters. Write the words.

table	sick	1. _____
loud	ladder	2. _____
finger	spoon	3. _____
home	print	4. _____
day	speaker	5. _____
step	dreams	6. _____

sea	time	7. _____
winter	print	8. _____
hand	shore	9. _____
snow	shake	10. _____
life	flake	11. _____
foot	time	12. _____

Word List

1	**2**	**3**	**4**
completely difference	absence temperature	especially spontaneous	category accidentally
equipped business	guarantee recommend	occurred fascinating	privilege advertisement

---

A. Write the missing letters.

1. complet __ __ __
2. equ __ __ __ ed
3. di __ __ erence
4. bus __ __ ess

5. absen __ __
6. g __ __ rantee
7. temperatu __ __
8. reco __ __ end

9. esp __ __ __ ally
10. o __ __ ur __ ed
11. spontan __ ous
12. fa __ __ inating

13. cat __ __ ory
14. priv __ __ __ ge
15. a __ cidentally
16. advertis __ ment

B. Unscramble these words. Write them. Find them in the wordsearch.

1. comeerndm _____
2. fenceredif _____
3. tanafiscgin _____
4. eatenarug _____
5. insubses _____
6. pedpiueq _____
7. pomceteyll _____
8. egroytac _____
9. sceneba _____
10. selliaycep _____

```
c a t e g o r y l p x c
b c f x d d x v e a u o
g u a r a n t e e g a m
w e s p e c i a l l y p
a e c i e c z y z x r l
b f i g n d f l b o f e
s g n s d e k d u d e t
e l a e t e s f z e t e
n s t w c q v s v z k l
c d i f f e r e n c e y
e l n r e c o m m e n d
z q g e q u i p p e d n
```

C. Write 10 words from the word list using these letters. You can use a letter more than once.

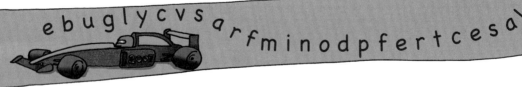

e b u g l y c v s a r f m i n o d p f e r t c e s a l

1. _____
2. _____
3. _____
4. _____
5. _____
6. _____
7. _____
8. _____
9. _____
10. _____

D. Make 3 small words from each word below. You can mix up the letters.

1. fascinating   2. accidentally   3. guarantee   4. category   5. completely

saint _____   _____   _____   _____   _____

_____   _____   _____   _____   _____

_____   _____   _____   _____   _____

E. Crossword.

Across

4. Happened.

7. Happens naturally.

8. Supplied with the necessary items for a task.

Down

1. A commitment that the product will work.

2. Suggest it to someone because you think it is good.

3. Buying and selling goods.

5. A group of similar items.

6. Makes the heart grow fonder.

F. ✗ the 8 incorrect spellings. Write them correctly.

1. difference ☐
2. temperature ☐
3. equiped ☐
4. fasinating ☐
5. ocured ☐
6. recommend ☐
7. spontaneous ☐
8. gaurantee ☐
9. especially ☐
10. privelage ☐
11. completely ☐
12. catigory ☐
13. accidently ☐
14. absense ☐
15. business ☐
16. advertisement ☐

_____
_____
_____
_____
_____
_____
_____
_____

G. Write the missing words. Use the word list.

1. The mountaineer set off, properly _____ .

2. An unusual thing _____ on the way to the match.

3. The librarian felt the book did not fall into any _____ .

4. The _____ between twenty and eleven is nine.

5. The audience burst into _____ applause.

6. The _____ was withdrawn because of numerous complaints from viewers.

7. The _____ was thirty degrees centigrade.

8. I thought the film was poor. I wouldn't _____ it.

9. The washing machine came with a five year _____ .

10. My uncle's company has gone out of _____ .

Phonics: ory, ary

Word List

❶	❷	❸	❹
history factory	category directory	secretary ordinary	library temporary
memory victory	territory compulsory	necessary voluntary	military dictionary

A. Write the missing letters.

1. __ __ st __ __ __ __
2. me __ or __
3. __ __ __ cto __ __
4. vi __ __ ory

5. cat __ __ ory
6. __ __ rr __ tory
7. __ __ __ ectory
8. com __ __ lsory

9. sec __ __ __ ary
10. __ __ __ essary
11. ord __ __ ary
12. vol __ __ tar __

13. li __ __ a __ __ __
14. __ __ lita __ __
15. tem __ __ __ ary
16. __ ictiona __ __

B. Make 3 small words from each word below. You can mix up the letters.

1. history   2. factory   3. military   4. victory   5. category

<u>sit</u>   _____   _____   _____   _____

_____   _____   _____   _____   _____

_____   _____   _____   _____   _____

C. Crossword.

Across

4. A compilation of word definitions.
5. Nothing special.
6. A building where things are made.
7. Recollection.

Down

1. A building containing books that may be borrowed.
2. Study of past events.
3. One's own choice.

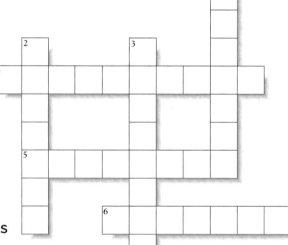

D. Remove a letter (or letters) to make a new word.

1. ~~memory~~ = <u>my</u>
2. victory = _____
3. directory = _____

4. history = _____
5. ordinary = _____
6. library = _____

7. factory = _____
8. military = _____
9. category = _____

E. Write the missing words. Use the word list.

1. I'm going to the _____ to borrow a book about space travel.

2. My older sister does _____ work for our local animal shelter.

3. My favourite subject in school is _____.

4. Our local _____ makes computer screens.

5. It is _____ to wear a seat belt in a car.

6. A tomcat marks his _____.

7. The dentist put a _____ filling in my tooth.

8. I needed a definition for a word so I looked up a _____.

9. We won the match because of an 'own goal'. It was a hollow _____.

10. My painting for the competition is in the ten to twelve year old _____.

F. Unscramble these words. Write them. Find them in the wordsearch.

1. lrabriy _____
2. mryliait _____
3. toarcyf _____
4. rteocgay _____
5. isohrty _____
6. roaluvtny _____
7. erymom _____
8. aesrnscey _____
9. yicotrv _____
10. rpoaytmer _____

y	x	q	i	h	p	g	o	z	a	i	y
z	w	n	x	k	g	d	l	r	a	o	c
r	p	q	x	f	a	c	t	o	r	y	y
u	o	t	e	m	p	o	r	a	r	y	m
z	z	b	n	b	i	x	w	j	l	h	e
n	j	q	t	u	s	l	x	y	y	i	m
l	i	b	r	a	r	y	i	q	e	s	o
c	a	t	e	g	o	r	y	t	v	t	r
z	u	n	u	u	u	r	u	x	a	o	y
v	o	l	u	n	t	a	r	y	o	r	l
o	m	n	e	c	e	s	s	a	r	y	y
v	i	c	t	o	r	y	s	n	c	n	i

G. Write the word list in alphabetical order.

1. category
2. _____
3. _____
4. _____
5. _____
6. _____
7. _____
8. _____
9. _____
10. _____
11. _____
12. _____
13. _____
14. _____
15. _____
16. voluntary

H. Match the letters. Write the words.

cat	ory	1. _____
volun	orary	2. _____
mem	egory	3. _____
his	tary	4. _____
temp	ary	5. _____
secret	tory	6. _____

lib	itory	7. _____
ordin	tory	8. _____
terr	itary	9. _____
mil	rary	10. _____
direct	ary	11. _____
fac	ory	12. _____

Commonly Misspelled Words

Word List

❶	❷	❸	❹
strength extremely	suspicious official	schedule conscience	definitely orchestra
apartment jewellery	ridiculous benefit	eliminate discipline	primitive unnecessary

A. **Write the missing letters.**

1. stren __ __ h
2. apart __ __ __ t
3. extrem __ __ y
4. jew __ __ __ ery

5. suspici __ __ s
6. rid __ __ __ lous
7. o __ __ ic __ __ l
8. ben __ f __ t

9. s __ __ edule
10. eli __ __ __ ate
11. consci __ __ ce
12. di __ __ ipline

13. def __ __ itely
14. pr __ __ __ tive
15. or __ __ __ stra
16. unneces __ ary

B. **Unscramble these words. Write them. Find them in the wordsearch.**

1. eftineb _____
2. eeetrxylm _____
3. onccseicen _____
4. trpmiiiev _____
5. ttenghsr _____
6. cliaiffo _____
7. plciisdnie _____
8. ywjeellre _____
9. torcheras _____
10. piousicssu _____

```
e  q  s  u  s  p  i  c  i  o  u  s
q  o  c  o  n  s  c  i  e  n  c  e
d  i  s  c  i  p  l  i  n  e  o  t
x  x  p  n  o  y  f  z  l  x  f  s
n  g  a  k  t  x  s  b  j  t  f  b
f  y  f  q  s  d  j  y  g  r  i  e
o  r  c  h  e  s  t  r  a  e  c  n
p  r  i  m  i  t  i  v  e  m  i  e
x  w  o  h  r  s  z  y  v  e  a  f
n  j  y  q  w  f  y  i  u  l  l  i
j  e  w  e  l  l  e  r  y  y  i  t
s  t  r  e  n  g  t  h  u  h  z  n
```

C. **Write 10 words from the word list using these letters. You can use a letter more than once.**

sapocibrtgfeymehdnildvatfi

1. _____   3. _____   5. _____   7. _____   9. _____
2. _____   4. _____   6. _____   8. _____   10. _____

D. **Make 3 small words from each word below. You can mix up the letters.**

1. extremely   2. apartment   3. discipline   4. orchestra   5. ridiculous

   meet _____   _____   _____   _____

_____   _____   _____   _____   _____

_____   _____   _____   _____   _____

E. Crossword.

Across

1. Musical group.
3. Soldiers are famous for it.
5. An inner moral voice.
6. Relating to authority.
7. If you feel this about someone, you feel they cannot be trusted.
8. A timetable or programme of things that are to happen.

Down

2. Silly, foolish.
4. Live in a simple way, without modern inventions and ideas.

F. ✗ the 8 incorrect spellings. Write them correctly.

1. suspicous ☐
2. schedule ☐
3. disipline ☐
4. strengh ☐
5. eliminate ☐
6. definiteily ☐
7. jewellry ☐
8. primitive ☐
9. offisial ☐
10. conscience ☐
11. apartment ☐
12. ridiculous ☐
13. unecessary ☐
14. extremly ☐
15. orchestra ☐
16. benefit ☐

_____
_____
_____
_____
_____
_____
_____
_____

G. Write the missing words. Use the word list.

1. The television autumn _____ was released.
2. A penalty shoot-out was held to _____ a team.
3. The _____ starter fired the gun and the marathon got under way.
4. 'I will _____ be there,' shouted Nora to her friend.
5. 'You look _____ in that hat,' the clown exclaimed.
6. The string section of the _____ were superb.
7. The _____ had a south-facing kitchen.
8. _____ does not always mean physical _____.
9. Having a _____ means knowing what is right or wrong.
10. The _____ was scattered on the pavement after the robbery.

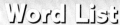

Word List

❶		❷		❸		❹	
pharmacy	physical	telephone	dolphin	triumph	photograph	phrase	microphone
paragraph	autograph	nephew	alphabet	sphere	geography	orphan	phantom

A. Write the missing letters.

1. __ __ arma __ y
2. para __ ra __ __ __
3. __ __ __ __ sic __ l
4. auto __ __ aph
5. __ __ leph __ ne
6. ne __ __ ew
7. dol __ __ in
8. __ __ __ __ __ __ abet
9. __ __ ium __ __ __
10. __ __ __ __ ere
11. photogr __ __ __
12. __ __ __ ograph __
13. __ __ __ ra __ __
14. __ __ __ ph __ __
15. micropho __ __
16. ph __ __ t __ __ __

B. Make 3 small words from each word below. You can mix up the letters.

1. dolphin   2. nephew   3. triumph   4. sphere   5. autograph

lion _____   _____   _____   _____   _____

_____   _____   _____   _____   _____

_____   _____   _____   _____   _____

C. Crossword.

Across

2. A group of sentences covering one idea.
6. A picture captured by a camera.
7. A child whose parents have died.
8. Contains 26 letters.

Down

1. A great victory.
2. Ghost.
3. A person's signature.
4. A small group of words.
5. A round, solid object.

D. Remove a letter (or letters) to make a new word.

1. dolphin = pin
2. orphan = _____
3. nephew = _____
4. alphabet = _____
5. autograph = _____
6. geography = _____
7. sphere = _____
8. phrase = _____
9. phantom = _____

E. Write the missing words. Use the word list.

1. I managed to get the actor's _____.

2. My brother keeps repeating a _____ from a television show.

3. Mum bought a bottle of cough medicine at the _____.

4. I was standing at the end of a pier when a _____ swam by.

5. We had a class _____ taken the other day.

6. The Greek _____ is different to the English one.

7. My favourite subject in school is _____.

8. I read the first _____ of the book and it was very interesting.

9. I've to fill in all the _____ features of Spain on a blank map.

10. At the karaoke night I went up to the _____ and sang a song.

F. Unscramble these words. Write them. Find them in the wordsearch.

1. epesrh _____
2. hmpoatn _____
3. shapre _____
4. epnihomrco _____
5. paatorugh _____
6. ewnhpe _____
7. hidlnop _____
8. appgrraah _____
9. rpimtuh _____
10. eoeelpthn _____

s	p	h	e	r	e	v	k	q	a	d	y
x	k	v	r	b	f	o	i	v	u	t	t
u	m	u	o	m	k	l	s	m	t	e	l
s	l	p	h	r	a	s	e	i	o	l	p
k	d	o	l	p	h	i	n	c	g	e	h
u	d	m	q	u	c	l	t	r	r	p	a
o	z	z	v	i	u	j	p	o	a	h	n
i	b	w	n	d	t	b	j	p	p	o	t
p	a	r	a	g	r	a	p	h	h	n	o
n	e	p	h	e	w	i	f	o	h	e	m
x	g	i	b	q	x	x	y	n	k	h	n
u	t	r	i	u	m	p	h	e	q	w	h

G. Write the word list in alphabetical order.

1. <u>alphabet</u>
2. _____
3. _____
4. _____
5. _____
6. _____
7. _____
8. _____
9. _____
10. _____
11. _____
12. _____
13. _____
14. _____
15. _____
16. <u>triumph</u>

H. Match the letters. Write the words.

dol	umph	1. _____
parag	ase	2. _____
sph	phin	3. _____
tri	raph	4. _____
geog	ere	5. _____
phr	raphy	6. _____

micro	graph	7. _____
or	tom	8. _____
alph	phone	9. _____
phys	abet	10. _____
photo	phan	11. _____
phan	ical	12. _____

Word List

❶		❷		❸		❹	
interrupt	describe	sincerely	peculiar	probably	controlled	particular	souvenir
expense	humorous	reference	shepherd	pitiful	unique	obstacle	satellite

A. Write the missing letters.

1. int _ _ _ upt
2. expen _ _
3. d _ _ cribe
4. hum _ _ ous

5. s _ _ _ erely
6. ref _ _ _ nce
7. pec _ _ _ _ r
8. she _ _ erd

9. prob _ _ ly
10. pit _ _ _ _
11. contro _ _ ed
12. un _ _ _ e

13. partic _ _ ar
14. ob _ _ _ acl _
15. s _ _ ven _ r
16. sat _ _ _ ite

B. Unscramble these words. Write them. Find them in the wordsearch.

1. cupleria _____
2. penexes _____
3. robblayp _____
4. ovunesri _____
5. redsbcei _____
6. botcasel _____
7. rinceeyls _____
8. uuienq _____
9. errptutin _____
10. ehderhsp _____

```
i z q v q v k n l q a a
f e t m g p g n s y o s
p r o b a b l y i z o h
f c c r e x p e n s e e
u n i q u e p c c a f p
p e c u l i a r e l t h
o b s t a c l e r j t e
r o u v c h w s e a d r
d e s c r i b e l n b d
s o u v e n i r y v t z
i n t e r r u p t a m e
p b a q b b h u q e e j
```

C. Write 10 words from the word list using these letters. You can use a letter more than once.

b u q r x p i h v t n e c f l s d o y

1. _____
2. _____
3. _____
4. _____
5. _____
6. _____
7. _____
8. _____
9. _____
10. _____

D. Make 3 small words from each word below. You can mix up the letters.

1. particular
   capital
   _____
   _____

2. satellite
   _____
   _____
   _____

3. reference
   _____
   _____
   _____

4. humorous
   _____
   _____
   _____

5. interrupt
   _____
   _____
   _____

E. Crossword.

Across

1. One of a kind.
6. Give information about.
7. Directed the behaviour of.
8. The cost incurred.

Down

2. Stop the flow.
3. Carries a crook!
4. Deserving of a lot of sympathy.
5. It can get in the way.

F. ✗ the 8 incorrect spellings. Write them correctly.

1. peculiar ☐	9. souvenier ☐	_____
2. sincerely ☐	10. discribe ☐	_____
3. pityful ☐	11. unique ☐	_____
4. sheperd ☐	12. humorous ☐	_____
5. expence ☐	13. probabley ☐	_____
6. controlled ☐	14. obstacel ☐	_____
7. interrupt ☐	15. reference ☐	_____
8. particuler ☐	16. satellite ☐	_____

G. Write the missing words. Use the word list.

1. 'Don't _____ me,' snapped the angry lady.
2. The starving and lame puppy was a _____ sight.
3. The leading hurdler knocked the final _____.
4. They received their television images via a _____ dish.
5. She brought home a fridge magnet as a holiday _____.
6. The _____ watched his flock at night.
7. The diamond was _____; there was only one of its kind.
8. The librarian directed her to the _____ section.
9. It was a _____ sight, the lion and tiger playing together.
10. He spoke so _____ that you were sure he meant it.

Word List

distance ❶ entrance	romance ❷ ignorance	sentence ❸ patience	violence ❹ experience
balance nuisance	advance ambulance	evidence difference	silence confidence

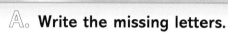

A. Write the missing letters.

1. dist __ __ __ __
2. __ __ __ ance
3. en __ __ anc __
4. __ __ isan __ __

5. rom __ __ ce
6. __ __ van __ __
7. ign __ __ anc __
8. __ __ bul __ nce

9. __ __ nt __ nce
10. __ __ id __ __ ce
11. pat __ __ __ ce
12. di __ __ erence

13. __ __ ol __ __ ce
14. sil __ __ ce
15. ex __ __ rience
16. con __ __ dence

B. Make 3 small words from each word below. You can mix up the letters.

1. romance   2. entrance   3. sentence   4. advance   5. nuisance

<u>care</u> _____ _____ _____ _____

_____ _____ _____ _____ _____

_____ _____ _____ _____ _____

C. Crossword.

Across

1. Causing annoyance.
7. A set of words that make sense.
8. Opposite to 'exit'.
9. Self-assurance.

Down

2. Without sound or noise.
3. Associated with love.
4. Move forward.
5. Even distribution of weight.
6. How far away an object or place is.

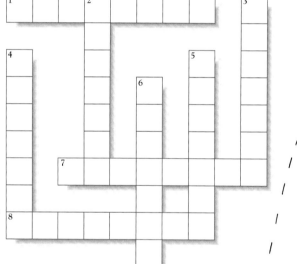

D. Remove a letter (or letters) to make a new word.

1. advance = <u>dance</u>
2. balance = _____
3. distance = _____
4. difference = _____
5. patience = _____
6. violence = _____
7. romance = _____
8. entrance = _____
9. evidence = _____

1. Within minutes of the accident happening, the _____ arrived.

2. There wasn't enough _____ to convict the prisoner.

3. Saint Valentine's Day is a special day for _____.

4. The _____ to the hotel was very impressive.

5. The acrobat lost her _____ and landed in the safety net.

6. My dad is a professional long _____ runner.

7. The only card game I know is called _____.

8. Going camping was a really enjoyable _____.

9. My baby sister can be a _____ but I love her dearly.

10. The teacher asked us to put the word 'patience' in a _____.

F. **Unscramble these words. Write them. Find them in the wordsearch.**

1. nleiesc   _____
2. edfirecfne   _____
3. cofecinden   _____
4. evdecine   _____
5. ornagneic   _____
6. ecnntese   _____
7. eaticpne   _____
8. eaistndc   _____
9. ceanmor   _____
10. nacublema   _____

x	s	b	l	o	p	f	d	j	b	h	e
p	p	a	t	i	e	n	c	e	m	t	d
c	o	n	f	i	d	e	n	c	e	t	a
w	d	i	f	f	e	r	e	n	c	e	m
p	u	u	h	c	c	k	g	p	s	v	b
j	c	v	e	p	t	i	y	i	i	i	u
d	i	s	t	a	n	c	e	g	l	d	l
s	e	n	t	e	n	c	e	e	e	e	a
i	g	n	o	r	a	n	c	e	n	n	n
i	i	r	o	m	a	n	c	e	c	c	c
j	b	w	v	e	l	u	x	z	e	e	e
c	j	i	s	m	g	e	n	i	h	l	f

G. **Write the word list in alphabetical order.**

1. advance   5. _____   9. _____   13. _____
2. _____   6. _____   10. _____ 14. _____
3. _____   7. _____   11. _____ 15. _____
4. _____   8. _____   12. _____ 16. violence

H. **Match the letters. Write the words.**

sil	erence	1. _____	confid	ance	7. _____
pat	tence	2. _____	ent	ience	8. _____
diff	ance	3. _____	exper	lence	9. _____
bal	ence	4. _____	vio	rance	10. _____
ignor	ience	5. _____	evi	ence	11. _____
sen	ance	6. _____	rom	dence	12. _____

Homophones

Word List

❶	❷	❸	❹
threw bow	profit principal	practise council	current stationery
through bough	prophet principle	practice counsel	currant stationary

A. Write the missing letters.

1. thr __ __
2. __ __ __ ough
3. b __ __
4. __ ou __ __

5. pro __ __ __
6. __ __ __ ph __ t
7. pr __ __ cipa __
8. __ rin __ i __ le

9. pr __ __ __ ise
10. __ __ acti __ __
11. coun __ __ __
12. __ __ __ __ sel

13. curr __ __ __
14. __ __ __ __ __ ant
15. st __ tion __ ry
16. stat __ __ __ ary

B. Crossword.

Across

1. __ __ __ __ __ __ __ __ __ __ makes perfect!
4. A strong flow.
6. Bend your body.
7. Give advice.
8. One who fortells events.

Down

1. I am going to __ __ __ __ __ __ __ __ playing the guitar.
2. Going in one side and out the other.
3. The head of a school.
4. An official body of people.
5. Propelled an object.
6. '... when the __ __ __ __ __ breaks, the cradle will fall.'

C. Write a sentence for each word.

1. through _____
2. bow _____
3. profit _____
4. principal _____
5. practise _____
6. counsel _____
7. stationary _____
8. current _____

D. Write the word list in alphabetical order.

1. bough
2. _____
3. _____
4. _____
5. _____
6. _____
7. _____
8. _____
9. _____
10. _____
11. _____
12. _____
13. _____
14. _____
15. _____
16. through

E. Read the clues. Write the word. Find it in the wordsearch.

1. Body of water moving in one direction. current
2. Main branch of a tree. _____
3. Financial gain. _____
4. Person with the highest authority. _____
5. A small dried fruit. _____
6. _____ makes perfect.
7. A fundamental truth. _____
8. _____ what you preach.

```
k  i  x  p  l  f  p  x  p  v  a  g
f  p  r  i  n  c  i  p  a  l  p  j
p  j  h  g  a  w  t  q  o  l  r  v
z  f  k  r  h  l  x  g  u  p  a  k
p  r  a  c  t  i  c  e  o  r  c  o
c  u  r  r  e  n  t  p  a  o  t  f
p  r  i  n  c  i  p  l  e  f  i  a
c  u  r  r  a  n  t  j  o  i  s  k
b  o  u  g  h  u  s  w  b  e  s
i  o  h  l  r  c  t  t  l  p  b  g
```

F. Remove a letter (or letters) to make a new word.

1. principle = pipe
2. current = _____
3. practice = _____
4. through = _____
5. prophet = _____
6. council = _____
7. currant = _____
8. profit = _____
9. practise = _____

G. Write the missing words. Use the word list.

1. I _____ the ball to my brother but he dropped it.
2. The bird was _____ for a moment before flying off.
3. My piano lesson is next week so I need to _____.
4. I sold the plants I'd grown and made a _____ of 10%.
5. My beach ball was swept out to sea by a strong _____.
6. I decided on _____ not to sign the letter.
7. My mum works for the local county _____.
8. The prince had to _____ down before the king.

H. Make 2 small words from each word below. You can mix up the letters.

1. through — hot
2. practice
3. current
4. prophet
5. bough

63

Word List

①		**②**		**③**		**④**	
nation	education	location	invitation	ambition	subtraction	addition	decoration
station	fraction	relation	attraction	action	information	creation	conversation

A. Write the missing letters.

1. __ __ tion
2. st __ __ ion
3. educat __ __ __
4. fr __ __ __ ion

5. __ __ cati __ __
6. rel __ __ ion
7. __ __ __ itation
8. a __ __ raction

9. __ __ biti __ __
10. __ __ tion
11. subt __ __ ction
12. inf __ __ mation

13. __ __ __ __ iti __ n
14. cr __ __ __ __ ion
15. dec __ __ ation
16. convers __ tion

B. Make 3 small words from each word below. You can mix up the letters.

1. relation   2. location   3. attraction   4. information   5. decoration

train _____   _____   _____   _____

_____   _____   _____   _____   _____

_____   _____   _____   _____   _____

C. Crossword.

Across

2. A place where a train stops on a railway line.

5. A specific place.

6. A group of people united by common descent, language or history.

7. A verbal or written request for your attendance.

8. What you wish to do in life.

Down

1. The process of doing something.

3. Relevant facts.

4. Someone who is related to you.

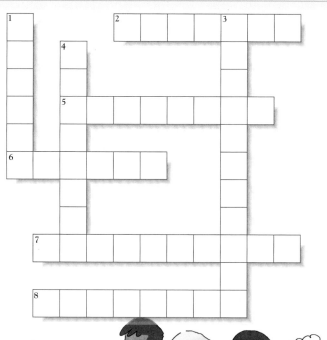

D. Remove a letter (or letters) to make a new word.

1. location = lion
2. addition = _____
3. decoration = _____
4. creation = _____
5. education = _____
6. ambition = _____

E. Write the missing words. Use the word list.

1. John, who's a _____ of mine, is coming for dinner.

2. I always found _____ to be easier than subtraction.

3. The climber described his exact _____ to the rescue team.

4. The bouquet of flowers was a beautiful _____.

5. Soon I will have completed my primary _____.

6. Eventually the train pulled out of the _____.

7. I received an _____ to my cousin's birthday party.

8. I surfed the internet for _____ about my favourite sport.

9. I had an interesting _____ with my granddad about modern music.

10. Only a _____ of the crowd turned up.

F. Unscramble these words. Write them. Find them in the wordsearch.

1. odiitadn _____

2. niretcao _____

3. otiastn _____

4. ooailtcn _____

5. oeiradoctn _____

6. oduaetcin _____

7. oriafnct _____

8. ntnviiaito _____

9. omiaibtn _____

10. oeanrtli _____

c	r	e	a	l	i	o	n	n	n	g	d
q	t	g	b	k	x	a	v	i	u	n	d
y	c	q	f	d	x	t	v	n	a	y	u
l	o	c	a	t	i	o	n	v	b	t	w
a	d	e	c	o	r	a	t	i	o	n	n
q	d	f	e	d	u	c	a	t	i	o	n
s	k	d	x	r	o	d	n	a	d	o	b
i	c	n	i	f	r	a	c	t	i	o	n
z	a	m	b	i	t	i	o	n	i	z	g	u
r	e	l	a	t	i	o	n	o	g	s	x
f	s	t	a	t	i	o	n	n	h	d	t
n	n	c	b	r	e	d	n	s	j	p	f

G. Write the word list in alphabetical order.

1. <u>action</u>

2. _____

3. _____

4. _____

5. _____

6. _____

7. _____

8. _____

9. _____

10. _____

11. _____

12. _____

13. _____

14. _____

15. _____

16. <u>subtraction</u>

H. Match the letters. Write the words.

act	ation	1. _____
fra	tion	2. _____
educ	ion	3. _____
add	ction	4. _____
stat	ition	5. _____
na	ion	6. _____

conver	ition	7. _____
infor	raction	8. _____
loca	sation	9. _____
amb	tion	10. _____
decor	mation	11. _____
att	ation	12. _____

Word List

❶		❷		❸		❹	
section	position	lotion	population	correction	condition	function	multiplication
caution	operation	situation	collection	detention	promotion	solution	competition

A. Write the missing letters.

1. sec _ _ _ _ _
2. _ _ _ _ tion
3. pos _ _ ion
4. _ _ er _ tion

5. _ _ _ ion
6. sit _ _ tion
7. _ _ _ _ ulation
8. _ _ _ ll _ ction

9. co _ _ ection
10. _ _ _ _ ention
11. con _ _ _ _ ion
12. _ _ _ _ _ otion

13. _ _ _ _ _ tion
14. sol _ _ _ on
15. _ _ _ ltiplication
16. com _ _ _ tition

B. Make 3 small words from each word below. You can mix up the letters.

1. section   2. caution   3. lotion   4. position   5. operation

<u>toes</u> _____ _____ _____ _____

_____ _____ _____ _____ _____

_____ _____ _____ _____ _____

C. Crossword.

Across

5. Warning.

6. A part of something.

7. Location.

8. A thick, smooth liquid.

Down

1. Purpose.

2. Answer to a problem.

3. The state of something.

4. Compulsory delay.

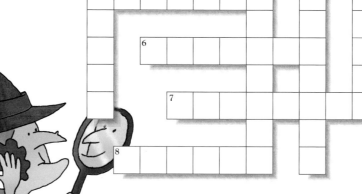

D. Remove a letter (or letters) to make a new word.

1. l~~o~~tion = <u>lion</u>
2. operation = _____
3. caution = _____
4. detention = _____
5. situation = _____
6. position = _____
7. function = _____
8. section = _____
9. solution = _____

E. Write the missing words. Use the word list.

1. I couldn't find a _____ to the algebra problem.
2. My favourite topic in maths is _____.
3. The _____ of our town is fifteen thousand people.
4. The roads were icy so Mum drove the car with extreme _____.
5. My cousin had an _____ on his foot but he's fine now.
6. I'm going to enter my painting in the art _____.
7. A _____ of the motorway was closed due to roadworks.
8. My mum was given a _____ in her job.
9. The day was very hot so I used lots of suntan _____.
10. There was a _____ outside the supermarket for the Red Cross.

F. Unscramble these words. Write them. Find them in the wordsearch.

1. inucftno   _____
2. onisulto   _____
3. noecptmtoii   _____
4. toasuinti   _____
5. cetoloclin   _____
6. oneetindt   _____
7. irnotpomo   _____
8. opuoilaptn   _____
9. noitocdni   _____
10. isipotno   _____

s	o	l	u	t	i	o	n	j	c	f	p
j	v	c	p	m	w	c	d	p	o	u	o
q	j	m	h	o	t	t	c	q	n	n	p
r	c	e	k	z	s	v	e	r	d	c	u
h	i	k	j	y	b	i	d	n	i	t	l
d	v	k	e	u	c	i	t	x	t	i	a
k	j	v	e	l	o	t	z	i	i	o	t
c	o	m	p	e	t	i	t	i	o	n	i
c	o	l	l	e	c	t	i	o	n	n	o
s	i	t	u	a	t	i	o	n	z	z	n
p	r	o	m	o	t	i	o	n	m	y	i
d	e	t	e	n	t	i	o	n	l	r	s

G. Write the word list in alphabetical order.

1. *caution*
2. _____
3. _____
4. _____
5. _____
6. _____
7. _____
8. _____
9. _____
10. _____
11. _____
12. _____
13. _____
14. _____
15. _____
16. *solution*

H. Match the letters. Write the words.

sol	ation	1. _____
prom	ition	2. _____
oper	ution	3. _____
caut	otion	4. _____
compet	ction	5. _____
fun	ion	6. _____

condi	ention	7. _____
sit	ation	8. _____
sect	tion	9. _____
popul	ition	10. _____
pos	uation	11. _____
det	ion	12. _____

67

UNIT 1 Spelling Check

1	2
3	4
5	6
7	8
9	10
11	12
13	14
15	16

16
15
14
13
12
11
10
9
8
7
6
5
4
3
2
1

How did you do?

Excellent ☐   Good ☐

Very Good ☐   Need to Improve ☐

UNIT 2 Spelling Check

1	2
3	4
5	6
7	8
9	10
11	12
13	14
15	16

16
15
14
13
12
11
10
9
8
7
6
5
4
3
2
1

How did you do?

Excellent ☐   Good ☐

Very Good ☐   Need to Improve ☐

UNIT 3 Spelling Check

1	2
3	4
5	6
7	8
9	10
11	12
13	14
15	16

16
15
14
13
12
11
10
9
8
7
6
5
4
3
2
1

How did you do?

Excellent ☐   Good ☐

Very Good ☐   Need to Improve ☐

UNIT 4 Spelling Check

1	2
3	4
5	6
7	8
9	10
11	12
13	14
15	16

16
15
14
13
12
11
10
9
8
7
6
5
4
3
2
1

How did you do?

Excellent ☐   Good ☐

Very Good ☐   Need to Improve ☐

UNIT 5 Spelling Check

❶	❷
❸	❹
❺	❻
❼	❽
❾	❿
⓫	⓬
⓭	⓮
⓯	⓰

16
15
14
13
12
11
10
9
8
7
6
5
4
3
2
1

How did you do?

Excellent ☐   Good ☐

Very Good ☐   Need to Improve ☐

UNIT 6 Spelling Check

❶	❷
❸	❹
❺	❻
❼	❽
❾	❿
⓫	⓬
⓭	⓮
⓯	⓰

16
15
14
13
12
11
10
9
8
7
6
5
4
3
2
1

How did you do?

Excellent ☐   Good ☐

Very Good ☐   Need to Improve ☐

UNIT 7 Spelling Check

❶	❷
❸	❹
❺	❻
❼	❽
❾	❿
⓫	⓬
⓭	⓮
⓯	⓰

16
15
14
13
12
11
10
9
8
7
6
5
4
3
2
1

How did you do?

Excellent ☐   Good ☐

Very Good ☐   Need to Improve ☐

UNIT 8 Spelling Check

❶	❷
❸	❹
❺	❻
❼	❽
❾	❿
⓫	⓬
⓭	⓮
⓯	⓰

16
15
14
13
12
11
10
9
8
7
6
5
4
3
2
1

How did you do?

Excellent ☐   Good ☐

Very Good ☐   Need to Improve ☐

UNIT 9 Spelling Check

1.
2.
3.
4.
5.
6.
7.
8.
9.
10.
11.
12.
13.
14.
15.
16.

| 16 |
| 15 |
| 14 |
| 13 |
| 12 |
| 11 |
| 10 |
| 9 |
| 8 |
| 7 |
| 6 |
| 5 |
| 4 |
| 3 |
| 2 |
| 1 |

How did you do?

Excellent ☐   Good ☐

Very Good ☐   Need to Improve ☐

UNIT 10 Spelling Check

1.
2.
3.
4.
5.
6.
7.
8.
9.
10.
11.
12.
13.
14.
15.
16.

| 16 |
| 15 |
| 14 |
| 13 |
| 12 |
| 11 |
| 10 |
| 9 |
| 8 |
| 7 |
| 6 |
| 5 |
| 4 |
| 3 |
| 2 |
| 1 |

How did you do?

Excellent ☐   Good ☐

Very Good ☐   Need to Improve ☐

UNIT 11 Spelling Check

1.
2.
3.
4.
5.
6.
7.
8.
9.
10.
11.
12.
13.
14.
15.
16.

| 16 |
| 15 |
| 14 |
| 13 |
| 12 |
| 11 |
| 10 |
| 9 |
| 8 |
| 7 |
| 6 |
| 5 |
| 4 |
| 3 |
| 2 |
| 1 |

How did you do?

Excellent ☐   Good ☐

Very Good ☐   Need to Improve ☐

UNIT 12 Spelling Check

1.
2.
3.
4.
5.
6.
7.
8.
9.
10.
11.
12.
13.
14.
15.
16.

| 16 |
| 15 |
| 14 |
| 13 |
| 12 |
| 11 |
| 10 |
| 9 |
| 8 |
| 7 |
| 6 |
| 5 |
| 4 |
| 3 |
| 2 |
| 1 |

How did you do?

Excellent ☐   Good ☐

Very Good ☐   Need to Improve ☐

UNIT 13 Spelling Check

1. _____
2. _____
3. _____
4. _____
5. _____
6. _____
7. _____
8. _____
9. _____
10. _____
11. _____
12. _____
13. _____
14. _____
15. _____
16. _____

16 15 14 13 12 11 10 9 8 7 6 5 4 3 2 1

How did you do?

Excellent ☐ Good ☐
Very Good ☐ Need to Improve ☐

UNIT 14 Spelling Check

1. _____
2. _____
3. _____
4. _____
5. _____
6. _____
7. _____
8. _____
9. _____
10. _____
11. _____
12. _____
13. _____
14. _____
15. _____
16. _____

16 15 14 13 12 11 10 9 8 7 6 5 4 3 2 1

How did you do?

Excellent ☐ Good ☐
Very Good ☐ Need to Improve ☐

UNIT 15 Spelling Check

1. _____
2. _____
3. _____
4. _____
5. _____
6. _____
7. _____
8. _____
9. _____
10. _____
11. _____
12. _____
13. _____
14. _____
15. _____
16. _____

16 15 14 13 12 11 10 9 8 7 6 5 4 3 2 1

How did you do?

Excellent ☐ Good ☐
Very Good ☐ Need to Improve ☐

UNIT 16 Spelling Check

1. _____
2. _____
3. _____
4. _____
5. _____
6. _____
7. _____
8. _____
9. _____
10. _____
11. _____
12. _____
13. _____
14. _____
15. _____
16. _____

16 15 14 13 12 11 10 9 8 7 6 5 4 3 2 1

How did you do?

Excellent ☐ Good ☐
Very Good ☐ Need to Improve ☐

UNIT 17 Spelling Check

1.
2.
3.
4.
5.
6.
7.
8.
9.
10.
11.
12.
13.
14.
15.
16.

16
15
14
13
12
11
10
9
8
7
6
5
4
3
2
1

How did you do?

Excellent ☐   Good ☐

Very Good ☐   Need to Improve ☐

UNIT 18 Spelling Check

1.
2.
3.
4.
5.
6.
7.
8.
9.
10.
11.
12.
13.
14.
15.
16.

16
15
14
13
12
11
10
9
8
7
6
5
4
3
2
1

How did you do?

Excellent ☐   Good ☐

Very Good ☐   Need to Improve ☐

UNIT 19 Spelling Check

1.
2.
3.
4.
5.
6.
7.
8.
9.
10.
11.
12.
13.
14.
15.
16.

16
15
14
13
12
11
10
9
8
7
6
5
4
3
2
1

How did you do?

Excellent ☐   Good ☐

Very Good ☐   Need to Improve ☐

UNIT 20 Spelling Check

1.
2.
3.
4.
5.
6.
7.
8.
9.
10.
11.
12.
13.
14.
15.
16.

16
15
14
13
12
11
10
9
8
7
6
5
4
3
2
1

How did you do?

Excellent ☐   Good ☐

Very Good ☐   Need to Improve ☐

UNIT 21 Spelling Check

❶
❷
❸
❹
❺
❻
❼
❽
❾
❿
⓫
⓬
⓭
⓮
⓯
⓰

| 16 |
| 15 |
| 14 |
| 13 |
| 12 |
| 11 |
| 10 |
| 9 |
| 8 |
| 7 |
| 6 |
| 5 |
| 4 |
| 3 |
| 2 |
| 1 |

How did you do?

Excellent ☐   Good ☐

Very Good ☐   Need to Improve ☐

UNIT 22 Spelling Check

❶
❷
❸
❹
❺
❻
❼
❽
❾
❿
⓫
⓬
⓭
⓮
⓯
⓰

| 16 |
| 15 |
| 14 |
| 13 |
| 12 |
| 11 |
| 10 |
| 9 |
| 8 |
| 7 |
| 6 |
| 5 |
| 4 |
| 3 |
| 2 |
| 1 |

How did you do?

Excellent ☐   Good ☐

Very Good ☐   Need to Improve ☐

UNIT 23 Spelling Check

❶
❷
❸
❹
❺
❻
❼
❽
❾
❿
⓫
⓬
⓭
⓮
⓯
⓰

| 16 |
| 15 |
| 14 |
| 13 |
| 12 |
| 11 |
| 10 |
| 9 |
| 8 |
| 7 |
| 6 |
| 5 |
| 4 |
| 3 |
| 2 |
| 1 |

How did you do?

Excellent ☐   Good ☐

Very Good ☐   Need to Improve ☐

UNIT 24 Spelling Check

❶
❷
❸
❹
❺
❻
❼
❽
❾
❿
⓫
⓬
⓭
⓮
⓯
⓰

| 16 |
| 15 |
| 14 |
| 13 |
| 12 |
| 11 |
| 10 |
| 9 |
| 8 |
| 7 |
| 6 |
| 5 |
| 4 |
| 3 |
| 2 |
| 1 |

How did you do?

Excellent ☐   Good ☐

Very Good ☐   Need to Improve ☐

UNIT 25 Spelling Check

1 2
3 4
5 6
7 8
9 10
11 12
13 14
15 16

16
15
14
13
12
11
10
9
8
7
6
5
4
3
2
1

How did you do?

Excellent ☐   Good ☐
Very Good ☐   Need to Improve ☐

UNIT 26 Spelling Check

1 2
3 4
5 6
7 8
9 10
11 12
13 14
15 16

16
15
14
13
12
11
10
9
8
7
6
5
4
3
2
1

How did you do?

Excellent ☐   Good ☐
Very Good ☐   Need to Improve ☐

UNIT 27 Spelling Check

1 2
3 4
5 6
7 8
9 10
11 12
13 14
15 16

16
15
14
13
12
11
10
9
8
7
6
5
4
3
2
1

How did you do?

Excellent ☐   Good ☐
Very Good ☐   Need to Improve ☐

UNIT 28 Spelling Check

1 2
3 4
5 6
7 8
9 10
11 12
13 14
15 16

16
15
14
13
12
11
10
9
8
7
6
5
4
3
2
1

How did you do?

Excellent ☐   Good ☐
Very Good ☐   Need to Improve ☐

UNIT 29 Spelling Check

1   2

3   4

5   6

7   8

9   10

11   12

13   14

15   16

16 15 14 13 12 11 10 9 8 7 6 5 4 3 2 1

How did you do?

Excellent ☐   Good ☐

Very Good ☐   Need to Improve ☐

UNIT 30 Spelling Check

1   2

3   4

5   6

7   8

9   10

11   12

13   14

15   16

16 15 14 13 12 11 10 9 8 7 6 5 4 3 2 1

How did you do?

Excellent ☐   Good ☐

Very Good ☐   Need to Improve ☐

UNIT 31 Spelling Check

1   2

3   4

5   6

7   8

9   10

11   12

13   14

15   16

16 15 14 13 12 11 10 9 8 7 6 5 4 3 2 1

How did you do?

Excellent ☐   Good ☐

Very Good ☐   Need to Improve ☐

UNIT 32 Spelling Check

1   2

3   4

5   6

7   8

9   10

11   12

13   14

15   16

16 15 14 13 12 11 10 9 8 7 6 5 4 3 2 1

How did you do?

Excellent ☐   Good ☐

Very Good ☐   Need to Improve ☐

HALLOWE'EN Spelling Check

Based on Units done up to:

Hallowe'en

1.
2.
3.
4.
5.
6.
7.
8.
9.
10.
11.
12.
13.
14.
15.
16.

16
15
14
13
12
11
10
9
8
7
6
5
4
3
2
1

How did you do?

Excellent ☐   Good ☐

Very Good ☐   Need to Improve ☐

CHRISTMAS Spelling Check

Based on Units done up to:

Christmas

1.
2.
3.
4.
5.
6.
7.
8.
9.
10.
11.
12.
13.
14.
15.
16.

16
15
14
13
12
11
10
9
8
7
6
5
4
3
2
1

How did you do?

Excellent ☐   Good ☐

Very Good ☐   Need to Improve ☐

EASTER Spelling Check

1	**2**
3	**4**
5	**6**
7	**8**
9	**10**
11	**12**
13	**14**
15	**16**

Based on Units done up to:

Easter

16
15
14
13
12
11
10
9
8
7
6
5
4
3
2
1

How did you do?

Excellent ☐   Good ☐

Very Good ☐   Need to Improve ☐

SUMMER Spelling Check

1	**2**
3	**4**
5	**6**
7	**8**
9	**10**
11	**12**
13	**14**
15	**16**

Based on Units done up to:

Summer

16
15
14
13
12
11
10
9
8
7
6
5
4
3
2
1

How did you do?

Excellent ☐   Good ☐

Very Good ☐   Need to Improve ☐

Complete Word List

Unit 1	Unit 2	Unit 3	Unit 4	Unit 5
there	picnic	know	pier	crocus
could	magic	together	piece	daffodil
every	comic	laugh	priest	carnation
round	music	eight	niece	tulip
both	attic	would	fierce	geranium
does	panic	those	shield	orchid
goes	public	their	field	poppy
right	Arctic	don't	yield	dahlia
these	traffic	before	grief	chestnut
use	elastic	because	thief	birch
which	frantic	around	chief	maple
write	terrific	always	relief	cedar
your	magnetic	once	shriek	palm
myself	clinic	again	believe	yew
some	athletic	please	siege	poplar
been	fantastic	where	achieve	sycamore

Unit 6	Unit 7	Unit 8	Unit 9	Unit 10
bored	liar	yield	edge	pollution
board	pillar	jealous	hedge	recycle
grate	altar	violence	ledge	preserve
great	dollar	argument	wedge	reduce
steal	collar	condemn	judge	reuse
steel	cellar	simply	nudge	natural
allowed	beggar	visible	budge	habitat
aloud	burglar	cemetery	badger	ozone
sweet	grammar	harass	trudge	global
suite	sugar	fulfil	grudge	plentiful
medal	popular	worthwhile	bridge	endangered
meddle	vinegar	desperate	fridge	rainforest
beach	singular	exceed	pledge	scarce
beech	muscular	subtle	smudge	desert
course	regular	embarrass	lodger	environment
coarse	particular	thorough	dredge	landscape

Unit 11	Unit 12	Unit 13	Unit 14	Unit 15
vision	riddle	conductor	twice	mystery
omitted	middle	rocket	price	surgery
opportunity	scribble	hovercraft	entice	grocery
immediately	miracle	ferry	device	nursery
restaurant	obstacle	platform	notice	brewery
experience	portable	porter	police	bribery
permanent	valuable	station	service	flowery
intelligence	reliable	tourist	justice	showery
hypocrite	available	pedestrian	practice	jewellery
definition	invisible	passport	advice	cemetery
insurance	sensible	submarine	reduce	machinery
camouflage	possible	language	produce	discovery
irrelevant	terrible	foreign	replace	flattery
medicine	horrible	uniform	disgrace	slippery
performance	struggle	temperature	surface	monastery
mischievous	tremble	scenery	introduce	stationery

Unit 16	Unit 17	Unit 18	Unit 19	Unit 20
Latvia	union	hygiene	editor	special
Lithuania	onion	column	lawyer	social
Netherlands	million	valuable	mechanic	crucial
Hungary	opinion	success	professor	initial
Estonia	billion	nuisance	engineer	martial
Cyprus	champion	occasion	optician	facial
Romania	companion	necessary	scientist	partial
Brazil	accordion	loneliness	athlete	financial
Luxembourg	scorpion	proceed	chemist	especially
Poland	stallion	disease	librarian	essential
Egypt	junior	ignorance	secretary	torrential
Canada	senior	knowledge	journalist	impartial
Switzerland	inferior	physical	electrician	official
Australia	superior	generally	jockey	artificial
Russia	exterior	government	surgeon	confidential
Nigeria	interior	introduce	musician	influential

Complete Word List

Unit 21	Unit 22	Unit 23	Unit 24	Unit 25	Unit 26
distant	vertical	handshake	completely	history	strength
brilliant	sphere	daydreams	equipped	memory	apartment
ignorant	isosceles	everybody	difference	factory	extremely
servant	arc	footprint	business	victory	jewellery
pleasant	area	handmade	absence	category	suspicious
elephant	cylinder	wintertime	guarantee	territory	ridiculous
assistant	breadth	stepladder	temperature	directory	official
extravagant	kilometre	fingerprint	recommend	compulsory	benefit
silent	pyramid	snowflake	especially	secretary	schedule
accident	protractor	homesick	occurred	necessary	eliminate
excellent	diagonal	background	spontaneous	ordinary	conscience
confident	decimal	tablespoon	fascinating	voluntary	discipline
enjoyment	parallel	lifetime	category	library	definitely
student	capacity	seashore	privilege	military	primitive
violent	equation	thunderstorm	accidentally	temporary	orchestra
experiment	symmetry	loudspeaker	advertisement	dictionary	unnecessary

Unit 27	Unit 28	Unit 29	Unit 30	Unit 31	Unit 32
pharmacy	interrupt	distance	threw	nation	section
paragraph	expense	balance	through	station	caution
physical	describe	entrance	bow	education	position
autograph	humorous	nuisance	bough	fraction	operation
telephone	sincerely	romance	profit	location	lotion
nephew	reference	advance	prophet	relation	situation
dolphin	peculiar	ignorance	principal	invitation	population
alphabet	shepherd	ambulance	principle	attraction	collection
triumph	probably	sentence	practise	ambition	correction
sphere	pitiful	evidence	practice	action	detention
photograph	controlled	patience	council	subtraction	condition
geography	unique	difference	counsel	information	promotion
phrase	particular	violence	current	addition	function
orphan	obstacle	silence	currant	creation	solution
microphone	souvenir	experience	stationery	decoration	multiplication
phantom	satellite	confidence	stationary	conversation	competition